LEGACY OF EMPIRE

Legacy of Empire
A journey through British society

WERNER GLINGA

Translated by STEPHAN PAUL JOST

 MANCHESTER UNIVERSITY PRESS

Published by
Manchester University Press
Oxford Road, Manchester, M13 9PL, U.K.
Wolfeboro, N.H. 03894-2069, U.S.A.

First published in German as *Erben des Empire* by
Campus Verlag GmbH, Frankfurt/Main, West Germany, 1983
German edition © 1983 Campus Verlag GmbH
This translation © 1986 Stephan Paul Jost 1986

British Library cataloguing in publication data applied for

Library of Congress cataloging in publication data applied for

ISBN 0-7190-2262-X *cased*

Printed in Great Britain by Bell and Bain Ltd., Glasgow

Typesetting by Hems & Co., Cypress House, Turners Lane, Gillingham, Dorset

CONTENTS

I will not cease from mental fight,
Nor shall my sword sleep in my hand
Till we have built Jerusalem
In England's green and pleasant land.

WILLIAM BLAKE

CHAPTER ONE

The rich man
and the
myth of the gentleman

CLUBLAND: ST JAMES'S STREET AND PALL MALL

Every nation dreams its own dream and projects its desires into its own myths and models. British thinking has crystallized a picture of the gentleman as the ideal, civilized person. This picture penetrated some of the remotest corners of the world, and today it has even attained the status of a stereotype in the entertainment industry. The ideal of the gentleman has never been bindingly written down. Each generation has modified or extended it, according to its needs. The gentleman as an ideal figure is as contradictory as the society which has generated the idealized projection in the first place. This projection is an aristocratic one through and through, containing a series of social images: the benevolent feudal landlord; the superior military commander; the cultured aristocrat after his 'Grand Tour' (i.e. the obligatory educational journey of aristocrats); the colonial officer fighting foreign barbarities; the fine statesman in a world full of despots and tyrants.

The ideal of this gentleman incorporates a democratic element as well, however. Aristocratic titles and material possessions alone do not make a gentleman, but noble deeds do. But the democratic, classless ideal of the gentleman is so inextricably mingled with aristocratic ideals that the two are not perceived as antagonistic contradictions in

British thinking. Anyone might become a gentleman if he adapts to the ideal, in his clothing and gesticulation, in his choice of words as well as their pronunciation. The ideal of the gentleman has deeply penetrated bourgeois ideas about education and upbringing, and it seduces some employees living in miserable conditions to defiantly acquire 'A touch of class' with the help of mannerisms.

Yet a man of money and respectable descent is regarded as a true 'gentleman' by his own social class. All the others, those who became gentlemen by education and behaviour, merely represent shadows of this ideal—a shadow ridiculed by the circles of 'true' class. Nevertheless, the ideal of the gentleman has remained. Indeed, it continues to hold sway as a great ideological illusion in the imagination of the bourgeoisie. This is the other side of British consciousness of tradition and the cult of the past: behind the veil of democracy there are reminders of a barbarous age when the division of people into masters and servants seemed natural. Arrogance and condescension, feelings of superiority and male chauvinism are not the virtues of a democratic society. But even today people are being brought up in this spirit, in 'public schools' during youth or in 'gentlemen's clubs' during adulthood. Britain has never consciously broken with her past. Britain emphasizes the unbroken continuity of her national history, a history many centuries old. Royalty, aristocracy, class oppression at home and of foreign peoples abroad, are still largely seen through the tinted spectacles of the ruling classes. The history of simple people has largely been ignored.

It is quite astounding how institutions reflecting the past have remained intact. The gentlemen's clubs, for example, have retained the same locations, buildings, inventories and ethos. The stronghold of the gentlemen's clubs is the so-called 'clubland' in central London. The stately homes of distinguished clubs were erected in close proximity to each other, just as medieval guildsmen used to settle in the same street. Pall Mall and St James's Street form the heart of clubland. Gentlemen's clubs can look back on a history of nearly 300 years. The histories of the clubs and the careers of many British politicians as well as well-known personalities from the arts and sciences are closely intertwined. The clubs had developed from discussion groups in seventeenth century coffee houses, against the background of Oliver Cromwell's Revolution. They soon became exclusive institutions of the ruling classes. From the very beginning, their social function was to provide members with a framework of informality and continuity. Personal acquaintances of existing members formed the basis for the admission of new members. Why has the continuity of clubs lasted to this day?

The clubland of London is located very centrally indeed, symbolically close to the sites of power. The Houses of Parliament, government buildings and two Royal Palaces are situated to the south of clubland, and the exclusive area of Mayfair is to the north. Clubland consists of luxurious drawing-rooms, where the rich and powerful may meet for private conversation. At the turn of the century, the number of gentlemen's clubs peaked at approximately 200. About 40 exist today. The most famous ones are located in aforementioned Pall Mall and St James's Street. Together with Piccadilly, both streets were the favourite boulevards of the British aristocracy, conveniently placed in the west of the old city centre, near the old Royal Palace. The aristocracy created this new residential focus for itself after the City had curtailed the feudal power of royalty since the Revolution which had culminated in the decapitation of King Charles I. in 1649. Because Pall Mall joins St James's Street in a characteristic fashion at right angles, both streets are called 'dog's leg' in British gentlemen's 'ideolect'.

This 'understatement' of the upper classes is characteristically flippant. When the owner of a castle calls his property a 'humid hole', or when excessively wealthy people talk about 'sufficient earnings', then this typifies the cunning ways of the dominant who do not wish to provoke the anger of the dominated unnecessarily. This is the class-specific meaning of 'understatement'. The British ruling classes have mastered the art of understatement. Distinguished clothing, for example, should never look new, but rather a little used and worn out. Newly-acquired wealth is vulgar. Slight stammering is cultivated by some gentlemen. The art of understatement continues to be effective and continues to cause confusion.

The two main streets of clubland today are no longer quiet boulevards but important roads for traffic in central London. The actual clubs, however, remain: huge palatial buildings in Pall Mall, elegant estates in St James's Street. The gentlemen's clubs on Pall Mall were founded in the 'bourgeois' nineteenth century and those on St James's Street in the 'aristocratic' eighteenth century. This dichotomy is still valid, because the social composition of Pall Mall clubs today is predominantly bourgeois as opposed to the aristocratic predominance of St James's St clubs. Members of the latter may still be condescending to members of the former. This can be said to represent a bizarre continuance of the historic conflict between bourgeoisie and aristocracy. Although the two seventeenth century Revolutions in 1649 and 1688 broke the feudal power of royalty, they did not break its economic and political power. The aristocracy was capable of adapting rapidly to new capitalist conditions as well as capable of forming an alliance with the new bourgeoisie. Due to this early bourgeois victory, eighteenth century England was very much more democratic and liberal than continental European countries. Hence, many philosophers representing the age of Enlightenment (such as Voltaire and Lichtenberg) looked to England as a model. In this climate of power divided between aristocracy and bourgeoisie many institutions took shape which are characteristic of the structure of British parliamentary democracy even today.

In many ways, however, the English aristocracy remained superior and the bourgeoisie attained approximate parity only during the nineteenth century. The expansion of the colonial Empire was accompanied by the acquisition of great personal wealth by industrialists and financiers. Prior to the Napoleonic Wars there were hardly any bourgeois millionaires. After the complete colonization of India, their numbers rose rapidly: 27 in 1880; 60 in 1900; 101 after World War I; 153 in 1939. This development is representative for the increasingly prosperous bourgeoisie as a whole, although personal wealth of aristocratic landowners increased, too. It is estimated that the Duke of Westminster, towards the end of the nineteenth century, was even richer than the then richest American millionaire W. H. Vanderbilt. The Duke's family today still owns very considerable land and property in London. The law of increasing concentration of wealth even applies among the aristocracy: some aristocrats own nothing but their titles, whereas others became unbelievably rich.

Despite their peaceful coexistence, the aristocracy kept the bourgeoisie at a distance socially. Prior to World War I it was practically impossible for a businessman to become a member of one of the distinguished gentlemen's clubs. This applied also to lawyers, unless they were practising at higher courts. The snobbery of gentlemen is therefore directed not against the working class (from which they were and are worlds apart), but against unwelcome groups belonging to the ruling circles: the *nouveaux riches* and non-aristocrats who rise socially via industry, the civil service or the military, and who claim power. In Britain there is still an intricate and confusing social ladder, the gradations of which may fool the outsider and cause much difficulty to the aspirant social climber. One of the main functions of snobbery is informal control over 'social intruders'. Most club entrances do not possess name or number plates. This exemplifies the anti-democratic character of understatement: the arrogance of the powerful. The clubs concerned freely admit their motivation behind this sort of camouflage. Someone who does not know where the insiders meet has no right to enter.

The principle of personal acquaintances guarantees

exclusiveness. On a gentleman's visiting card, the private address is commonly shown in the left-hand corner and the name of his club in the right-hand corner. No club address is given. The oldest clubs like White's, Brooks's or Boodle's do not even add the word club. As an institution, White's is as known as the Bank of England or the Houses of Parliament. Taxi drivers do not just have to know the addresses of embassies, ministries and public offices but of gentlemen's clubs as well. Customers merely need to say Travellers, Athenaeum or Naval and Military to state their destination. The last line of *Who's Who* entries usually contains information concerning club membership. This may help to characterize the social status of the person in question. Membership in gentlemen's clubs often functions as a social passport. It would be slightly suspicious for a member of the establishment not to be member of a gentlemen's club as well.

The ruling circles' snobbery has found its way into national ideology and official custom. No British stamp, for example, states its country of origin. Clearly, the Queen's profile has to suffice for identification. The recipient would not be taken seriously if he or she was unable to identify the stamp. Apart from its actual social function, snobbery can be farcical. In 1980 'British Airways' decided to drop 'Airways' on its planes and retain the word 'British' only. The then chairman of the company Roy Watts justified this change by saying that the retention of the sole word 'British' would inspire customers with confidence, because 'British is best' in this area and 'British Airways' the best of Great Britain. At the beginning of 1985, this policy was reversed and the title 'British Airways' reappeared on the planes.

In particular journalists sometimes claim with amazing glibness that British institutions such as the police force, the BBC or Parliament are 'the best in the world'. Occasionally, this expression refers to such a variety of things, that it becomes empty. These kinds of statement show the power of 'gentlemen morality' on bourgeois thinking.

Aristocratic arrogance is distortedly reflected down the social scale.

The gentlemen's craving for recognition as well as their claim to power are clearly manifested in the architecture of their clubs. Club premises are amongst the most glamorous and beautiful in London. Pall Mall is dominated by nineteenth century bombastic classicism. Travellers and Reform Club resemble Italian Palazzi, renaissance-style. During the nineteenth century, the architectural taste of urban princes in Italy served as a model for British industrialists. Rich wool barons, like Yorkshiremen Titus Salt and Samuel Lister, had palatial spinning mills built. Both were knighted for services rendered to the woollen industry. The megalomania accompanying the expanding Empire made the official architecture in the cities more and more pompous. The premises of the Royal Automobile Club could be taken for a state residence, for instance. The club buildings in St James's Street seem quite modest in comparison. Their style is authentic: typical eighteenth century aristocratic country mansions. Both the interior and the exterior of Brooks's and Boodle's are designed according to aristocratic family estates of the time. Eighteenth century dimensions are smaller than nineteenth century ones, and the atmosphere is more private. Ground-floor bay-windows are quite special, because they represent the architectural expression of a particular social behaviour. From bay-windows club members could observe distinguished ladies and gentlemen walking past the club. The bow-window in White's served as an ideal position for the leading dandy of the Regency period (around 1810), Beau Brummel, to pass verdicts about the standards of aristocratic clothing.

The inside of gentlemen's clubs is also quite reminiscent of a squire's or a gentleman's country mansion. Boodle's houses magnificent paintings displaying horses and huntings. Boodle's morning room on the ground floor is very spacious indeed and contains large leather armchairs and leather sofas. It is purposely furnished to cater for dealing with private correspondence and reading newspapers. Every gentlemen's club has its own letterhead paper and offers desks to write on. There are still letters printed in *The Times* or the *Daily Telegraph*, which give the sender's club address. Boodle's showpiece is the drawing room on the first floor. Decorative stuccowork on the ceiling, wall paintings with Greek and Roman motives as well as a marble fireplace have been constructed in the style of architect Robert Adam. Adam was one of the leading exponents of classicist architecture in Great Britain. The dining-room in Boodle's is called the 'coffee-room', as it is in every gentlemen's club. This is because public coffee houses in the seventeenth century were the immediate forerunners of private clubs. Traditionally, no coffee is served in 'coffee-rooms', one of the many rituals which have been complacently kept.

THE FRENCH REVOLUTION, THE REGENCY PERIOD AND THE DANDY

There are two further eighteenth century clubs in St James's Street which are not only famous but also played an important role in the political history of the United Kingdom: White's and Brooks's. In increasingly sharp social conflicts towards the end of the eighteenth century, the confrontations between the two great aristocratic groupings, the Whigs and the Tories mirrored the class struggles of the epoch. White's developed to be the headquarters of the 'new Tories' under the leadership of William Pitt the Younger. Brooks's became the focal point for the Whigs led by Charles James Fox. Tories and Whigs did not represent political parties in today's sense. Members of both factions kept changing sides. Alliances were formed more on the basis of bribery than political conviction. However, both Pitt the Younger and Charles James Fox represented two sharply contrasting political positions, in which the later development of the Conservative Party (from the Tories) and the Liberal

Party (from the Whigs) is prefigured. Pitt stood for expansionist colonial policies under the direction of the state (as opposed to private trading companies). Pitt was furthermore supposed to be the main architect of the coalition against Napoleonic France. Fox, by contrast, sympathized with the ideas of French Enlightenment and welcomed the outbreak of the French Revolution. A 1796 caricature by James Gillray may still be seen in Brooks's, *The impending terrors of the French invasion.* This caricature is a piece of anti-revolutionary propaganda of that time, directed against the Whigs under Fox. After 1789, brutally repressive measures were implemented to oppress all Republican associations as well as revolutionary thought. The caricature features White's and Brooks's as venues for this national confrontation. They attain symbolic significance for the old regime and revolutionary camp, respectively, albeit seen from a royalist perspective. Revolutionary guards carrying the banner *Vive la République* can be seen. St James's Palace, which is burning in the background, was obviously set on fire by the guards. The first aristocrats have already been hung on lanterns and White's is in the process of being stormed, as it represents a vital citadel of royalist Tories. The first gentlemen are being pushed from the balcony. At Brooks's opposite, supporters of the revolutionary party are equipped with a guillotine. Three people have already been decapitated for the public good, according to a nearby scroll. At the centre of action, however, there are Fox (in common clothing) and Pitt (in aristocratic clothing). As leader of the revolutionary party, Fox is striking Pitt, who is tied up, with rods. The caricature as a whole may be regarded as a prime example of anti-revolutionary demagogy. Fox was not like Danton or Robespierre in any way. He was a liberal, enlightened aristocrat. Despite his sympathy with the French Revolution, he largely supported the *status quo* in England. Fox's importance was inflated: he was portrayed as the political head of republican ideas in order to brutally persecute the *real* disciples of revolutionary thought as criminals and traitors.

Historian E.P. Thompson points out in his work *The Making of the English Working Class* that coffee houses and taverns not only led to the development of distinguished gentlemen's clubs, but also to the formation of political circles among common people. Probably the most important of the latter was the *London Corresponding Society*, which is regarded as one of the first associations of the developing working class. The principal political objective of the *London Corresponding Society* was to achieve universal suffrage. By contrast with the exclusive gentlemen's clubs, conditions of membership were democratic and universal. Anyone who agreed with its political objectives could join the society. There was no upper limit to membership. The prohibition of the *London Corresponding Society* in 1794 and the concomitant arrest of its leading members initiated the period of anti-Jacobin persecution in England. This is the historical background to the mock fight between White's and Brooks's.

Soon, life in the gentlemen's clubs was once more devoted to rather more agreeable pursuits, despite the Napoleonic Wars. The so-called Regency period between 1800 and 1820 became a kind of *belle epoque* in British history. The rich seemed to have more money than ever before, war profits created new wealth overnight. French aristocrats escaping the Revolution brought previously unknown refinements to England. Fashionable new spas such as Cheltenham were constructed rapidly. The easygoingness, frivolity and incredible fashion-madness of the eighteenth century reached its zenith during Regency, before the Victorian age, with its sombre gothics and moral puritanism, disciplined society for new tasks necessitated by the world-wide colonial Empire. Regency created its own easy-going personality: the dandy. The dandy was a high-class professional impostor who did not swindle to support his extravagant lifestyle, but won the necessary cash at the gambling table. Mastery of card games was an indispensable part of his 'professional' training. Frequently of humble birth, the dandy immaculately acquired and perfectly performed the code of conduct as well as all relevant snobberies pertaining to the ruling circles. The king of Regency dandies, Beau Brummel, virtually dictated what was fashionable and what was not among the rich and noble. Accompanied by the princely household of aristocrat Jeunesse Dorée, he used to comment upon both the clothing and appearance of aristocrats passing White's bow-window, Brummel's favourite observation spot. His word was law. He was a friend of the Prince Regent. Brummel's morning toilet could have been confused with a royal levée, because it took place in the presence of a complete entourage. Lady Hester described such an occasion:

Sometimes he would have a dozen dukes and marquises waiting for him whilst he was brushing his teeth or dressing himself, and would turn round with the utmost coolness and say to them: 'Well, what do you want? Don't you see I am brushing my teeth?' Then he would cry: 'Oh! there's a spot–ah! it's nothing but a little coffee. Well, this is an excellent powder, but I won't let any of you have the receipt for it.'   (Chancellor, 1922, p. 241.)

This section of society did not work. It was wholly pre-occupied with receptions, games and clothing. This was the usual life-style of aristocrats, but it must have been a tough job for dandies. Beau Brummel, for instance, incurred tremendous debts, which is why he had to escape from England. He died impoverished in France, mentally deranged.

The dandy is preserved in the ideal of the gentleman. Sons of wealthy parents still cultivate the eccentricity of the dandy in gentlemen's clubs. They consciously revive the past by preserving aristocratic mannerisms. They wear silk hats and grow whiskers and address each other with pompous titles, some of which will actually be inherited from their fathers. This masquerade is dismaying precisely because it does not reflect historic reminiscences, but is a morbid expression of power structures still in existence.

Our knowledge about the personal origins, financial transactions and private lives of historical dandies has been greatly expanded by a recent, fortuitous finding. The private trunk of dandy Scrope Berdmore Davies was discovered in 1976 down in the vaults of Barclay's Bank in Pall Mall. The trunk was full of private notes, unknown hymns by Shelley and precious lyrical manuscripts by Lord Byron, a friend of Berdmore Davies. In 1820 Davies fled from his creditors. Before leaving for Belgium, he deposited his documents with Barclay's Bank which kept the trunk (unopened) in custody ever since. Davies was a man-about-town, humorous, a playboy, and hell-bent on gambling. Lord Byron remarked of his circle of friends: 'He always beat us in the battle of words, and his eloquence not only delighted us but held us together.' Davies did not leave his brilliance to chance, however. A notebook filled with literary quotations was found in his trunk. Witty utterances seem to have been memorized for appropriate occasions. Education and intelligence were necessary means to compensate for lack of noble descent. Money, too, was essential. Davies had been educated in Eton and Cambridge. During his Eton days, he practised games of dice and cards and bet for money. While at Cambridge, he gained access to London's high society (via Lord Byron). Davies' desire for an easy life in the midst of rich and privileged friends must have developed during his time at public school. His parental home hardly prepared or predestined him for this. His father was a priest in the country, and he had ten brothers and sisters. But family connections and a scholarship enabled Davies to go to Eton in 1794, thereby entering an entirely different world. Old bills from this time document how he learnt to dress himself better, buy things on credit, employ servants and entertain friends in pubs. Similar circles in Cambridge (1802–1807) were the next step. Davies then went to London together with Lord Byron and led a dissolute life for the following two years. Lord Byron was heavily in debt, too, and this and other reasons made him leave England in 1809. Dandies were in their element in the gentlemen's clubs. Davies was a member of several, including Brooks's. He did not succeed, however, in being admitted to White's, even then the most prestigious of clubs.

Games of cards and betting for money had begun to dominate club life some time before Regency. Some clubs were known as gambling dens as early as the mid eighteenth century. Stakes were incredibly high. Some players won or lost literally a fortune during the course of a single night. Horace Walpole, whose comprehensive correspondence vividly chronicled many aspects of eighteenth century life, wrote in 1770 that young gentlemen lost ten, fifteen or twenty thousand pounds in Club Almack on *one* night. At that time, a shopkeeper earning an *annual* salary of £100 was considered well-to-do. Head clerks in big trading companies made about £50 per annum, whereas teachers and workers had only £20 a year. In Almack's, minimum stakes of £50 per game were regularly stipulated. The entire amount of money per table could well be in the region of £10,000. An 1872 guide-book *Clubs and Club Life in London* by John Timbs illustrated in some detail the attitude and manner of some participant players:

The play was certainly high—only for the rouleaus of 50 *l.* each, and generally there was 100,000 *l.* in specie on the table. The gamesters began by pulling off their embroidered clothes, and put on frieze greatcoats, or turned their coats inside outwards for luck. They put on pieces of leather (such as are worn by footmen when they clean the knives) to save their laced ruffles; and to guard their eyes from the light, and to prevent tumbling their hair, wore high-crowned straw hats with broad brims, and adorned with flowers and ribbons; masks to conceal their emotions when they played at quinz. Each gamester had a small neat stand by him, to hold his tea; or a wooden bowl with an edge of ormolu, to hold the rouleaus.
(Timbs, 1872, pp. 72–3.)

The great politicians of the time, like Fox, Pitt and

Wilberforce (who acted as the parliamentary spokesman for the opponents of slave trade), were all clubmen and players. According to Brooks's housebook, a gentlemen called Mr Thynne abruptly discontinued his membership on 21 March 1772 since he had won only £12,000 during the past two months. It was furthermore reported that Fox played Mr Fitzpatrick on one occasion from 10 p.m. until 6 p.m. the following afternoon without interruption. A servant had to indicate whose turn it was next as the two gentlemen were too sleepy to follow. Fox frequently made huge profits, often more than £8,000 on a single night. There were occasions, however, when he lost his entire hoard.

By contrast with aristocratic club clients, dandies did not have huge resources at their disposal. Scrope Berdmore Davies' fast life in London meant he had to risk every-thing—all the time. He needed enormous sums of money to support his lifestyle, and therefore had to risk similar sums of money to get them. His principal sources of income were playing games of cards and dice in the club, as well as betting on horse races in Newmarket. These old personal documents reveal his then well-kept financial secret. The rise and fall of Scrope Berdmore Davies were equally rapid. In 1814 he enjoyed a streak of good luck and owned more than £22,000, which would have easily sufficed to support himself comfortably the rest of his days. However, his wealth declined to about £5,000 in 1816. Then he had luck again. His friend Hobhouse noted in his diary on 11 April 1816 that Scrope went to his club after dinner and won £3,700 on the night. Despite good beginnings, the year 1817 brought loss after loss. In Club Watiers he lost £1,050 on 11 September, £995 on 13 September and £105 on 15 September. Although he won £270 the next day, his account at Watiers still remained £1,110.13s. in the red. Scrope had several bank accounts, and he trans-ferred the same sum of money several times in order to demonstrate his liquidity (a practise which has not been forgotten). But both Scrope's career as dandy and the

Regency period itself were drawing to a close, irrestibly. His lost stake in a horse race at Newmarket was probably the last straw. All possible deceitful manoeuvres had been exhausted and nobody was prepared to lend him any more money. Only escape into exile could save him from certain incarceration. He was only thirty-eight years old. During the first days of 1820, Scrope Berdmore Davies bid farewell to his friends and fled to Belgium. He lived in Ostend for several years and later in Paris, where he managed to entertain people with endless stories of his magnificent time in Regency London. He announced the publication of his memoirs but they never appeared.

In some ways the dandy served as a kind of court-jester of high society. It was he rather than society who was the fool in the end. Regency dandies such as Scrope Davies seemed to personify the attempt of the revolutionary bourgeoisie to refine its revolutionary impetus by aping the aristocracy. Scrope Davies, for example, supported the French Revolution, admired Napoleon and actively participated in a committee set up by the radical democratic politician Sir Francis Burdett MP. Sir Francis was left of the Whig Party. Furthermore, by professional vocation, Scrope Davies belonged to the intelligentsia of his time. He was educated at Eton and later became a fellow of King's College in Cambridge. He regularly spent several months of the year there. At that time, however, teaching and research were in a sorry state and university teachers enjoyed very little social esteem. But Scrope Davies was mainly interested in the lifelong salary connected with the award of fellowship. The appointment brought the additional advantage of being close to the horse races in Newmarket. Which type of intellectual did Scrope Berdmore Davies embody? Was he a bourgeois revolutionary, who was rendered ineffective by society as a dandy and ruined by hedonism? Perhaps this interpretation goes a little far. In the dandy the bourgeois was courting public favour in a society, which–deep down– he repudiated and rejected. However, with Scrope's escape to the Continent this age in England comes to an end.

The year 1819 furthermore represents a landmark in the history of the British labour movement. On St Peter's Field near Manchester between 50,000 and 80,000 workers gathered at an open-air mass meeting in order to demand economic and parliamentary reforms. After Napoleon's defeat, the working class appears as an independent entity for the first time. They no longer demanded reforms as members of political circles but as members of a new social class. The rally at St Peter's Field on 16 August 1819 was dispersed by force. Eleven civilians died and hundreds were injured. In ironical reference to the battle of Waterloo, these events were termed the *Peterloo massacre*, which became a symbol for the repression of democratic demands. The protest actions of the developing working class finally signalled to the middle classes that reforms were best carried out in close cooperation with the old order only. The bourgeoisie sealed their alliance with the aristocracy and proved to be both loyal and reactionary. As far as personal contact was concerned, however, the bourgeois was rejected and humiliated by the aristocrat. Despite this, he copied the aristocratic way of life as much as possible. He furthermore enforced his own social separation from the working class even more ruthlessly than the aristocracy did.

SNOBS AND MIDDLE CLASSES

Changing times did not leave 'clubland' unaffected. In close proximity to St James's Street, the great nineteenth century clubs were erected in Pall Mall. These were dominated by the middle classes. Arts and sciences, too, created a representative building for themselves: the Athenaeum on Pall Mall. During the time of Dr Johnson's Literary Club they still met in taverns and coffee houses in the Covent Garden area. The Athenaeum was erected in Graeco-Roman style in 1830. Its portico is supported by double pillars, but dominated by a gold-plated, larger-than-life-sized statue of the Greek goddess Pallas Athene. The building possesses an official character. The name Athenaeum at the time designated a literary or philosophical society. The actual building is situated at the beginning of Pall Mall and provides a direct view onto Waterloo Place. It looks more monumental and magnificent than may be justified by its function as a venue for leading artists and scientists. The architecture of the building symbolized the complete integration of the intelligentsia in the existing power structure. The attraction and appeal of gentlemen's clubs for the bourgeois intelligentsia seems to be symptomatic of a general fascination exerted by the establishment. To this day the British ruling classes have been remarkably successful in attracting the support of the intelligentsia and indoctrinating it with the myth of the cultivated gentleman as a neutral ideal of civilization. The right-wing intellectual appears to be the rule in England. Also, in the ruling ideology social advancement seems inextricably bound with the acquisition of education and culture.

The history of the Athenaeum may provide examples of this. The physicist Michael Faraday was a founding member, like the writer Sir Walter Scott. Even the preamble to the Athenaeum's constitution embodied the alliance of the intelligentsia with the money-donating aristocracy. The relevant clause reads: 'The Athenaeum is instituted for the association of individuals known for their scientific or literary attainments, artists of eminence in any class of the fine arts, and noblemen and gentlemen distinguished as liberal patrons of Science, Literature, or the Arts.' (F.G. Waugh, 1968, pp. 4–5.) In this context it was not just money that was determining, but power as well. The first list of members (issued in founding year 1824) included not only the Prime Minister of the day, Lord Liverpool, but furthermore the names of six later Prime Ministers: Canning, Wellington, Peel, Russell, Aberdeen and Palmerston. It became a social distinction to be admitted to a gentlemen's club of this type. The votes on prospective new members were a popular topic for the gossip columns. Clubman and writer William Makepeace Thackeray, an acute observer of snobbish mannerisms, used to say that membership of the Athenaeum was at least as valuable as a degree from Oxford University. Young Charles Darwin became a member in 1838 on the recommendation of his colleague and mentor Charles Lyell. This was after his *Beagle* voyage, but long before the publication of his classic work on *The Origin of Species*. Darwin had always been a typical Victorian private scholar. Sufficiently wealthy to sustain himself without a permanent position, he was enthusiastic enough to pursue his scientific research projects almost single-handed for decades. Darwin felt overwhelmed when he visited the Athenaeum for the first time, aged 29. As he wrote to Charles Lyell: '. . . after the second half day is finished I go and dine at the Athenaeum like a gentleman, or rather like a lord, for I am sure the first evening I sat in that great drawing-room, all on a sofa by myself, I felt just like a duke. I am full of admiration at the Athenaeum, one meets so many people there that one likes to see. . .' (P. Brent, 1981, p. 240.)

Admission to membership in such a gentlemen's club did not just mean elevation to some kind of intellectual aristocracy (as alluded to by Darwin), it also meant being in touch with the leading circles of the time. One did not just become a mere member of some club, but a member of a much greater, invisible club of the *élite* of the nation.

William Makepeace Thackeray became a member of the Athenaeum in 1851. His first attempt to gain admission failed several years before. Thackeray poured scorn over the old gentlemen members who intensely disliked his satirical works, and who therefore had rejected his candidacy out of vengeance. But Thackeray felt hurt, too. Any member of London society could not just disregard the codes of conduct. Thackeray's intimate knowledge of these rules, however, enabled him to ridicule the snobbery of their bourgeois adepts. As a member of staff of the satirical magazine *Punch* he published a series of humorous contributions during 1846 and 1847, which came out as a collection in 1848 entitled *The Book of Snobs*. This book consists of a series of tableaux depicting various circles of society: the City; military; Court; Country; university and club. Thackeray illustrated in numerous anecdotes the social behaviour of the British class society of his age. The fundamental evil in this class-ridden society was the excessively refined aristocratic and bourgeois ranking order, ranging from the Royal family to the fishmonger. The appropriate handbook indicating the exact position of aristocratic families in this social pyramid is *Debrett's Peerage*, which is still published. Class-conscious families treat it as a second bible. This penetration of the entire society with a spirit of submissiveness towards aristocratic titles and the ideal of the gentleman was called *lordolatry* by Thackeray. *Lordolatry* had infected British society to such an extent that 'it might be impossible for any Briton not not be a snob in some way or another' (Thackeray, 1848). Thackeray told of Prince Albert of Saxe-Coburg, Queen Victoria's husband, that, when hunting, he always had his gun loaded by a servant especially employed for this purpose. After each shot, however, the Prince would not pass the gun straight back to his servant but to an accompanying nobleman who would then give the gun to the assistant. The royal hands were not supposed to touch those of the servant. And royal practice was emulated as much as possible at virtually every rung of the social ladder.

The basic evil, Thackeray continued, was the privileges of the aristocracy. 'Feudal, medieval superstition' dominated even universities. Aristocratic students wore clasps of gold and silver in order to signal their privileged status to everyone. They did not need to sit exams. They received their degrees after two years of study, for which ordinary students had to work seven years. Although Thackeray viewed these various manifestations of class society with great humour, he occasionally cannot disguise his anger: 'I cannot stand it any longer, this diabolical invention of gentility, which suffocates every natural friendliness or honest friendship. . . But hierarchy and succession of titles are a lie which should be thrown into fire.' (Thackeray, 1848, p. 528.)

Hallmarks of snobbery, according to Thackeray, were condescension towards the lower and subservience towards the higher classes. Society had produced 'the snob' as its archetype. The gentlemen's clubs were full of them; people who preferred pretence to truth. Clubs represented the ideal platform for snobs, a vanity-fair, which seemed to have been created for attracting the admiring eyes of others:

Yet how little you can tell from a man's outward demeanour! There's a man at our club—large, heavy, middle-aged—gorgeously dressed—rather bald—with lacquered boots—and a boa when he goes out; quiet in demeanour, always ordering and consuming a *récherché* little dinner, whom I have mistaken ford LORD POCKLINGTON[3] any time these five years, and respected as a man with five hundred pounds *per diem*; and I find he is but a clerk in an office in the City, with not two hundred pounds income, and his name is JUBBER. My LORD POCKLINGTON was, on the contrary, the dirty little snuffy man who cried out so about the bad quality of the beer, and grumbled at being overcharged threehalfpence for a herring.

(Thackeray, 1948, p. 178.)

Whereas Jubber likes to play the gentleman, an ideal which he actually cannot afford, the real gentleman, the Lord, behaves in a petty and impudent way—a manner which remains unredressed due only to his title.

In this aristocratic and bourgeois world the working class is hardly present. Personal contact is minimal. Subjectively speaking, the snob's main worry is competition within his own class, and the consolidation of his position within it. The snob endeavours to follow faithfully the unwritten rules of this world, in which he wants to rise. He reveals himself as being a snob whenever he makes a mistake in the 'correct' emulation of these rules. This may happen at any of the many twists and turns of the socially refined behavioural patterns, often simply because emulators lack the confidence of originators.

The informal barriers between the social groups are not always instantly apparent. Their effectiveness is based on the simple principle of personal acquaintance and recommendation. This applies, for example, to the admission of new members to gentlemen's clubs, where 'the old boys' network' attains great importance. Members of Boodle's and White's have to have been involved with the club for several years before they gain the right of suggesting new candidates (whom one also has to have known personally for years). This method reduces drastically the possibility of admitting unwanted members. There are additional hurdles. Suggested candidates are included on the list of applicants, but the candidacy is pursued further only if a considerable number of seconders can be found. Also, some clubs stipulate waiting periods of several years duration before the application for membership will be brought to a vote. During the nineteenth century this period could last up to ten years.

Not all gentlemen's clubs are able to afford such extreme exclusivity today. Although they continue to entertain the principle of personal sponsorship, they also admit new members on the recommendation of well reputed institutions. The united Oxford and Cambridge Universities' Club requires members to have studied at either Oxford or Cambridge, although academic success is not essential. The East India Club recruits public school leavers on the recommendation of the headmaster. Membership fees vary between £200 and £300 per year. Some gentlemen are of course members in several clubs. There are the so-called second clubs, like Pratt's and Beefsteak, which mainly serve as dining venues. The term 'second' does not imply inferior reputation. These clubs commonly comprise one or two large dining halls; and sociable aspects appear to have higher priority than in some of the conventional great clubs.

Traditionally, clubs catered for gentlemen only. Around

the turn of the century, many women's clubs developed but they did not last. Only one has survived: the University Women's Club, founded in 1886 for women possessing university education. Many gentlemen's clubs nowadays offer associate membership for members' wives. This does *not* mean, however, that the smoking-room, coffee-room, morning-room or the library were opened for their use. The actual club rooms stayed closed to women; they were usually given their own section in some side wing of the club building. On specified days and in the company of gentlemen, they could be taken to club lunch or dinner. A gentleman may of course enter women's rooms any time, the separation of sexes works only in one direction.

THE PUBLIC SCHOOL, THE FIRST CLUB IN THE LIFE OF A GENTLEMAN

Public schools are for children and teenagers what gentlemen's clubs are for adults. They are dominated by a similar class-specific exclusiveness. Most public schools are still not mixed. They foster the principle of 'boys only'. The public school represents the first 'compulsory' club in the life of a gentleman. An applicant during the nineteenth century had to be the 'son of a gentleman' to gain admission. It is not surprising that there have been some changes since then, but what is astounding is that the character of elitist schooling should have changed so little. The social aspects of public schooling are far-reaching and cannot be compared with state schooling.

These range from accent to clothing, gestures to table manners, personal connections to personal knowledge about the world of the powerful. Public school education smoothes the way to the professions. Public schools tend to be elitist organizations rather than straightforward schools. They provide their pupils with a class education and with class consciousness. Many gentlemen's clubs display the coat of arms of those public schools with which the club is associated. Certain families have been sending their children to the same public school for generations, just as fathers and sons have been members of the same gentlemen's club for generations.

The headmaster of Westminster Public School, John Rae, writes in his book *The Public School Revolution* (1981) that numerous reforms have transformed the character of public schools and he claims that they now bear little resemblance to the picture offered by Lindsay Anderson's film *If* (1968). The film depicts the public school as an institution of paramilitary discipline, generating an equivalent, violent rebellion in the pupils. Rae contends that this repressive character in the form of corporal punishment and orders to stay indoors have disappeared. A third of all public schools now admit girls, and the criteria of admission have been liberalized. The public school Harrow-on-the-Hill required until the 1960s a series of recommendations on behalf of every applicant, officially entitled 'Harrow references and connections'. This system was not unlike the admission procedure to gentlemen's clubs. Under 'connections' went, among other things, membership of the Church of England. John Rae claims that this kind of strict and formalized system of references has now ceased to exist. As proof he points out that the proportion of public school pupils of Jewish and Moslem creeds has risen. The admission of children from the ruling classes of the Third World, however, has little to do with democratization. This also applies to the improvement of the scholarship system directed to those pupils, whose parents cannot afford to pay fees of more than £3,000 per year per public school pupil. The mere possibility of children from lower class backgrounds rising socially has never changed the existence of classes themselves. John Rae admits, however, that public schools have returned to their old order and discipline after the revolt connected with the student movement of the late 1960s. 'If somebody who had been accepted into public school in 1960 were to repeat his education in 1980, he would probably encounter more that was familiar than unfamiliar.' (Rae, 1981, p. 111.) The author does not take seriously the plans of some Labour politicians to abolish public schools. This is not because he doubts the determination of Labour, but because he considers the ruling classes to be more powerful.

Despite all political change, the British ruling classes possess astonishing self-confidence in the preservation of the basic structure of obsolete elitist organizations. Only about 0.5 million out of an approximate total of 9 million male and female school pupils in England attend public schools. This figure includes all private primary and preparatory school pupils. This small minority finds itself in luxuriously equipped schools which most cities or local authorities just cannot afford. At Aldenham, for instance, one of the cheaper public schools, about 350 boys have at their disposal: an all-weather hockey ground with flood-lights; two squash courts; six covered courts for the ball game 'Eton five'; eight asphalted tennis courts; one shooting range and two heated swimming pools. Even ten-year-old public school pupils express themselves with such eloquence and precocity that they reveal their systematic education as 'gentlemen'. On the question of which career they would like to pursue, only the top professions are mentioned. Their way of speaking is already as arrogant and cynical as that of their fathers. In the quotation below a fourteen-year-old pupil of Westminster Public School talks about his professional goal:

I suppose I'll end up being a barrister like my father. It's always rather assumed I'm going to be one, or some sort of lawyer. It's quite a worthwhile job, father enjoys it. He is a Queen's Council, about fourth from the top. Father has lots of influential friends, it certainly might help. I've got a friend whose father was a court judge and he was a right honourable at about 35.   (Mack, 1977, p. 7.)

The question whether he was embarrassed by this kind of parental patronage clearly struck him as odd. He identified 'chauvinism' as the basis of his chosen profession;

he did so openly and without any scruples about the anti-democratic character of his views. 'Barristry is based on chauvinism', he said.

As arrogant and condescending as members of the ruling classes may be in company, their institutions endeavour to conceal their class character as much as possible. Public schools justify their existence with claims to provide educational excellence. It is advanced that more than 50 per cent of all students at Oxford and Cambridge previously attended public schools, implying that these prepare their pupils better for university studies than schools run by the state. This divide in the educational system leads to a deepening of the class divisions in the United Kingdom. Resources are distributed so unjustly that the state sector finds it very difficult to catch up this unfair advantage. This vicious circle cannot be broken without abolition of the educational divide itself: due to relatively enormous resources, public schools attract, on the whole, better pupils and better teachers who are therefore no longer available to the state sector. The consequence is that all people who depend on the state or the public sector for the improvement of their quality of life are increasingly disadvantaged. This does not just apply to the areas of education and health, but also to the economy itself. In this sense, the Conservative slogan 'less state' is a formula of reactionary propaganda, the realization of which would deprive all lower social strata of the means of improving their lot. It is part of the ideological achievement of the ruling classes that they have broadly succeeded in putting across a general association between 'private sector and higher standard' on the one hand and between 'public sector and lower standard' on the other. This phenomenon is not even discussed, let alone understood, as resulting from a class-ridden society. The great social questions of our time are dealt with in Britain, too, in a manner neutral of class, as if one were confronted by technological problems to which there are different expert solutions. This applies to a large extent to the idealized picture of the gentleman.

THE GENTLEMAN AS NOBLE KNIGHT AND SOCIAL PARASITE

The picture of the gentleman oscillates from the sublime to the ridiculous. This differentiation into two opposite assessments developed during the nineteenth century. During that time the myth of the gentleman was extended by several elements. An important addition was that the gentleman did not just represent the prototype of English civilization, but also the incarnation of western humanism. The gentleman became the successor to the Christian knight without fear or blemish. Cardinal Newman, one of the leaders of the Christian-philosophical Oxford move-ment of around 1840, defined the gentleman as 'a person who would never inflict any pain'. Art critic and social reformer John Ruskin talked in his work *Modern Painters* of the gentleman as possessing 'deep humanity' and 'natural subtlety'. At about the same time the perception of the gentleman as a comical or even ridiculous figure emerged. A representative description may again be found in Thackeray's *Book of Snobs* when the author character-izes the club gentlemen Wiggle and Waggle:

They come of the middle classes. One of them very likely makes believe to be a barrister, and the other has smart apartments about Piccadilly. They are a sort of second-chop dandies; they cannot imitate that superb listlessness of demeanour, and that admirable vacuous folly which distinguishes the noble and high-born chiefs of the race; but they lead lives almost as bad (were it but for the example), and are personally quite as useless.

(Thackeray, 1848, p. 183.)

This eccentric and idle image of the gentleman was quickly adopted abroad. On the Continent, the English gentleman was perceived as a noble if eccentric lord on his 'grand tour' right until the period of Romanticism. From the mid nineteenth century onwards, however, he became a figure of ridicule. One of the best satires of the English gentleman of the nineteenth century was written by Jules Verne. His novel *Around the World in Eighty Days* is simply the portrayal of an eccentric gentleman who, during the usual chat about current affairs took up a bet to travel around the globe in eighty days. Here is the initial description of the novel's hero:

In 1872 No. 7, Savile Row, Burlington Gardens, the former home of Sheridan, was occupied by Mr Phileas Fogg. He belonged to the Reform Club of London, and although he never did anything to attract attention he was one of its most unusual and conspicuous members. Of this enigmatic personage, indeed, nothing was known except that he was a fine gentleman of good breeding. He had a certain resemblance to Byron, but a Byron with a moustache and side-whiskers, a Byron who seemed to be unaffected by circumstances, who could have lived a thousand years without growing old.

Undoubtedly English, Phileas Fogg might not have been a Londoner. He had never been seen on Exchange, nor at the Bank, nor in the City. No ships owned by him had ever entered the London docks. He had never taken part in the public administration. He had never been called to the Bar, nor had he pleaded in the Law Courts. He was neither manufacturer nor merchant nor gentleman farmer. He belonged to none of the Learned Societies.

Phileas Fogg was a Member of the Reform Club, and that was all. . .   (Jules Verne, 1967, p. 7.)

The perception of the gentleman therefore falls into two opposite extremes during the course of the nineteenth century: the noble knight versus the social parasite. It is one of the characteristics of ruling ideology to reconcile the most contradictory elements with each other. This does not point to a lack of logic but to a great deal of cunning, as well as to moral double standards. The ideal of the gentleman promises vices and virtues at the same time, which may each be activated according to the inclinations of the person concerned. If somebody today endeavours to be admitted to the circle of gentlemen, then he aspires to acquire the public reputation of being a noble knight while leading the private life of an idle layabout.

The type of non-employed gentleman of independent (although ill-defined) means appears also to have shaped the character of Sherlock Holmes. He shows clear signs of eccentricity, on the borderline between the sublime and the ridiculous. Dr Watson noticed with some astonishment that Holmes did not have the faintest idea about literature, philosophy and politics but that he could play the violin well (although only when under pressure). Furthermore, Holmes was very good at boxing and fencing. Satires emphasize an additional characteristic feature: amateurism. The gentleman is a true amateur in his pursuits which he, of course, masters professionally, but which he does not practise as a profession. Phileas Fogg's trip around the world illustrated this principle perfectly. Bourgeois emulation of the supposed virtue of amateurism has had disastrous consequences as well, leading to such bizarre phenomena as the 'gentleman capitalist' and the 'gentleman industrialist'. In a competitive world they often came to grief.

According to the myth, the gentleman possesses natural superiority unique to his background which enables him to get the upper hand in all situations in life and to excel in all fields. This ideal has been developed into an ideology and propagated in numerous works of fiction, devotional literature and adventure books. Generations of pupils from public and grammar schools devoured stories like *Broad Stone of Honour* by Kenelm Henry Digby, *Euphranor* by Edward Fitzgerald, *Tom Brown's Schooldays* by Thomas Hughes, *Past and Present* by Thomas Carlyle and *Westward Ho* by Charles Kingsley. The attribution of chivalrous decency, honesty as well as natural superiority to the image of the English gentleman helped to shape those leadership qualities and enthusiasm which the Empire needed for its expansion. Hence, the ideal of the gentleman formed part of colonial ideology during the nineteenth century. It furthermore helped to convince the huge army of colonial administrators of the rightfulness of

the colonial cause. It incited them to venture to all corners
of the world, even if this meant personal sacrifice, in order
to achieve their supposed civilizing mission.

The myth of the naturally superior gentleman was quite
often shattered by harsh realities. For example it could be
disastrous when the British military was confronted by an
equal and well equipped opponent. The gentlemen soldiers'
exaggerated feelings of superiority led to dreadful massacres
during World War I when officers ordered their troops—in
gross misjudgement of the military situation—into the
open machine-gun fire of the German lines. During World
War II the British lost two of their biggest aircraft carriers
in Singapore, because they did not believe the Japanese to
be capable of flying combat aircraft. They presumed
German pilots were operating in the cockpits. Class
prejudices and racial prejudices are closely connected.

The myth of the gentleman, however, arises again and
again like a phoenix from the ashes, ignoring defeat and
failure. A famous picture is on display in the Cavalry Club,
one of the gentlemen's clubs for officers, supposedly serving
as an example to the new generation. Painted in 1913 by
J.G. Doleman, it bears the title *A very gallant gentleman.*
On this painting, a muffled man is depicted battling with a
snowdrift. His hands, head and feet are thickly wrapped.
In the background, the contours of a tent are barely
discernible. He is bent forward and obviously mustering his
last strength to cope with the snowstorm. The portrait
shows Captain Lawrence Oates of the Inniskilling Fusiliers.
Lawrence Oates personified heroism to the World War I
generation attending public schools and military academies.
He sacrificed himself in order to rescue others. Oates
participated in the 1911–12 Antarctic expedition under
the leadership of Captain Robert Falcon Scott, an officer
of the Royal Marines. From 1901 to 1904 Scott led a
successful expedition to the icy sea surrounding the
Antarctic continent. On his return to Britain he was
welcomed as a national hero. *The Times* wrote in 1904:
'The example given by Commander Scott and his colleagues

in strength of character as well as self-sacrifice in the service of Science will undoubtedly help to keep the very spirit alive amongst us which contributed so much to England's greatness in the past.' In 1908 Scott was planning the triumph of his career: the hoisting of the Union Jack on the South Pole. This second expedition was not official, it arose from Scott's personal ambitions. It developed into a race between his group and that of Norwegian polar researcher Roald Amundsen who was simultaneously venturing to the South Pole. Scott reached the South Pole on 17 January 1912, one month after Amundsen. On the long march back, Scott and his colleagues succumbed to the cold. Even if they had succeeded in completing the last miles, they would have been crippled for life due to very severe frostbite affecting all limbs. The participants of this expedition did not possess sufficient food and had to pull their own, heavy sledges. It became clear to Captain Oates after a few weeks that he was unable to continue, suffering from frozen feet as well as physical exhaustion. He bid farewell to his companions, left the tent and trudged into the snowstorm. 'We knew', Scott reported in his diaries, 'that poor Oates was walking to his death.' Oates' dead body was never found. We only know about these events because Scott kept a diary later discovered underneath his head. Scott himself described Oates' self-sacrifice as the deed of a brave man and an English gentle-man. A few days after Oates' death, Captain Scott and his remaining two companions Dr Edward Wilson and Lieutenant Bowers lay down in the snow to await death themselves. Scott's last entry was not a very personal one. He invoked the national ideal to which he felt committed: 'We are very near the end of our journey, and I am finishing it in company with two gallant, noble gentlemen. . . But we have been to the Pole, and we shall die like gentle-men' (after Girouard, 1981, pp. 3–4).

When the dead bodies and the diary were found eight months later, a stone hill was erected and inscribed in memory of Captain Oates: 'Hereabouts died a very gallant gentleman, Capt. L.E.G. Oates, of the Inniskilling Fusiliers.'

Once the news of the deaths reached Britain, Scott and his companions were awarded the highest honours post-humously, and were mourned as national heroes. A memorial service was held in the presence of King George V. Questioning this legend means committing a grave offence even today. A critical biography of Captain Scott was published in 1980. It still caused indignation, although it has been known for a long time that Scott's expedition had been ill-prepared and was somewhat amateurish. Grave mistakes were made due to a lack of expertise. Amundsen's expedition, however, proceeded smoothly and successfully, because it had been planned and carried out professionally. Although Scott's attitude was heroic and courageous from an individual point of view, the race itself was a senseless act of heroism. The British architectural historian Mark Girouard wrote a study of the myth of the gentleman and the rejuvenation of ideals of chivalry entitled *The Return to Camelot*. Girouard commented on Scott's final diary entry that it 'suggests an attitude in which heroism becomes more important than the intelligent forethought which would make heroism unnecessary. In the code of the gentleman intelligence was a little suspect.' (Girouard, 1981, p. 14.)

Unbelievable amateurism was also responsible for a different catastrophe. Again, senseless competition was involved. Significantly, the tragedy in question took place at about the same time as Scott's abortive expedition. On 4 April 1912, the biggest and safest ocean liner of the world, the *Titanic*, pride of the British nation, collided with an iceberg on her maiden voyage. The *Titanic* sank within two hours and forty minutes. There were many rich and famous people on board. It might have to do with the national importance of the ship or with the fame of the passengers that heroic legends formed about alleged bravery and noblemindedness associated with the launch-ing of rescue boats. Survivors told tear-jerking stories which reflected the ideology of the gentleman. Colonel

John Jacob Astor, for instance, chivalrously accompanied his young bride to the rescue boats, bid farewell with a smile, raised his hand in military salute and then returned to the gentlemen who were staying behind. The newspapers referred to them as 'the knightly young heroes of the *Titanic*'. It was reported that a Mrs Douglas had begged her husband to join her in the rescue boat, only to receive the reply: 'I must be a gentleman'. The *Titanic* crew supposedly stayed at their posts until the last moment. All men were said to have faced the end with calmness and composure. Samuel Guggenheim and his butler allegedly appeared in the smoker's saloon of the first class, both in immaculate formal evening dress, declaring 'we have dressed in our best and are prepared to go down as gentlemen' (Girouard, 1981, p. 5).

Later investigations shed a somewhat different light on the sinking of the *Titanic*. In particular, gross negligence concerning elementary safety precautions became evident. Although there were 2,340 people on board, rescue boat facilities were available to 1,100 passengers only. It remained furthermore striking that despite a calm sea only 651 people were in fact brought to safety. No rescue exercises had been practised prior to the *Titanic*'s maiden voyage. Also, passengers and crew had not been designated certain rescue boats. Hence, the catastrophe was due not just to a blind belief in technology but also to a blind feeling of superiority and the captain's and officers' inflated opinions of themselves.

GENTLEMAN AND THE ARISTOCRACY TODAY

The myth of the confident and superior gentleman remains alive to this day. He still masters the difficulties of life almost without effort. He still solves the world's problems with elegance and style. In James Bond, Her Majesty's secret agent, Ian Fleming created a modern variant of the myth of the gentleman. James Bond normally wears bow-tie and formal dress, as if he were on the way to his club.

His boss, Sir Miles, is member of the gentlemen's club Blade's, a re-creation of the real club Boodle's. Ian Fleming was educated at Eton and at Sandhurst Military Academy. He also worked as a financier in the City of London and as a leading member of the news service during World War II. If even completely new realities are interpreted in the light of obsolete patterns, then national myths must be embedded deeply in people's way of thinking. The force of these 'modern' myths as with their ancient counterparts appears to cover reality with a veil of dreams and lies.

There is a recent example of how the myth of the gentleman aids in glossing over reality. At the beginning of May 1980 the paramilitary special branch SAS stormed the Iranian Embassy in London. Afterwards, the mass media were full of praise for the speed, precision and tidyness with which the action was carried out. A comedy sketch was subsequently televised, revealing, no doubt unconsciously, the classic 'myth of the gentleman interpretation' of the liberated embassy. A young couple is sitting in a restaurant, selecting their dinner from a menu. All of a sudden, there is a commotion. The doors are pushed open and soldiers occupy the restaurant. They tell the couple that a military coup has led to a change of government, and they would now serve the meal. Suddenly there is renewed uproar and guerilla fighters storm the restaurant. The military regime has been overthrown, they would serve dinner now. But chaos breaks out once more and Soviet soldiers enter and take over. The couple does not get round to eating. Then the last bang transforms the entire situation. All intruders disappear. A clean white table cloth descends from the ceiling. Two candles are put up, and delicious dishes are served. Finally there is calm. Two elegant gentlemen dressed in dark suits, white shirts and black bow-ties come in, light the candles and say 'with compliments from the SAS'. The audience responds with loud applause to this elegant solution to utter chaos. The gentleman still appears to be called for to bring about peace and quiet by the moral authority of his personality.

He has natural leadership qualities, even on the international scene. Just as during the time of the Empire, the British gentleman creates order in the barbarian chaos of the rest of the world.

How do British people themselves reflect on this national myth? A. Smythe-Palmer published an anthology entitled *The Ideal of a Gentleman* in 1908, a book meant to illustrate this 'magnificent character'. The author had compiled relevant essays for more than twenty years. The collection did not analyze ideology but propagated it. As a piece of devotional literature, it reflected the century-long process whereby the concept 'gentleman' came to be the myth of an entire nation, perhaps precisely because its definition and class character were vague. The ideology proclaims that everybody may become a gentleman, that it is a question of character rather than birth. Edmund Burke recorded in 1795 the then wide-spread opinion that the king can create a nobleman, but he cannot make a gentleman. Generations of bourgeois sons emulated this moral ideal. It may have even convinced them of the democratic character of British society, helping them to ignore the contempt and rejection shown by 'real' upper class gentlemen in personal encounters. Apologists of the myth assert even today that 'the gentleman' has nothing whatever to do with class division. Simple folk, however, quite early viewed the gentleman as a protagonist of the ruling classes. The famous verse of the 1381 Peasants' Revolt in England reveals this quite unmistakably: 'When Adam delved and Eve span who was then the gentleman?'

British opponents of the ruling system of society have never had any illusions about the class character of the concept 'gentleman'. George Bernard Shaw remarked in his *Maxims for Revolutionists*: 'A gentleman of our days is one who has money enough to do what every fool would do if he could afford it: that is, consume without producing.' (Shaw, 1971, p. 630.)

The specific course of events in the British class struggle enables one to understand the term 'gentleman' has come to contain both aristocratic and democratic elements. In the principle of understatement, the ruling aristocratic and middle classes have mastered the art of adaptation without actually giving up their privileges. They have been superb at concealing their true positions, at making concessions just in time, at retreating under pressure until the energies of the opponent were spent. They have furthermore exercised considerable persuasion. All of this has contributed to the absolutely astonishing continuity of British social and national history, unique in the world. There has been no revolution in Britain since 1688, despite the extreme exploitation and misery in the country during the industrial revolution. Adaptation to changing times as well as deliberate disguise are both very conscious principles of survival, often freely admitted ones. The royal publishers Debrett brought out a humorous handbook on the subject of 'gentlemen'. It reads in the preface: 'Nor is the species really vanishing—though elusive specimens of the present generation described in this book are nevertheless getting harder for the uninitiated to find outside a few select private zoos called clubs. The coming generation of English leopards are, as usual, and with long practice in camouflage, quietly engaged in adjusting their spots.' (Sutherland, 1978, p. xi.)

Will the British gentleman be able to save his skin forever more? There are approximately 7,000 ladies and gentlemen in the United Kingdom today, who may rightfully claim an aristocratic title. After the Royal Family the top section of the social pyramid is represented by (in that order) 25 dukes, 37 marquises, 173 earls, 110 viscounts and 438 barons. The continuance of royalty and aristocracy is not just a comical curiosity. This class has succeeded in acquiring new positions of power by adapting to capitalist economic structures. They have done so on the ruins of the old aristocratic power structures. Some aristocrats still own whole villages and districts in the most beautiful parts of the country. Even the feudal rights of medieval aristocracy have never been formally abolished. Parliamentary democracy in the United Kingdom developed in compromise with this class structure. The success of British parliamentary democracy is largely based on the creation of a balance between the classes rather than their abolition. If excessive wealth and inherited privileges still represent the true focus of social power, one must question whether parliamentary democracy has achieved fundamental social reforms.

W.D. Rubinstein published a study on the rich in the United Kingdom in 1981. In this work, the secrecy surrounding the world of wealth is emphasized. The author, who does not belong to the political left, draws the reader's attention to the new methods used to undermine fiscal legislation as well as to distort financial statistics. The only reliable data available come from the estate register. Although these estimates are far too low in many cases, an astounding trend is clearly discernible since the industrial revolution. The rich in today's Britain are richer than ever before: 'The most prosperous ladies and gentlemen in contemporary Britain possess wealth in excess of anything seen in the past, both in absolute and relative terms.' (Rubinstein, 1981, p. 234.)

More than 300,000 people in Great Britain hold assets exceeding £100,000. The super-rich command fortunes of astronomic, hardly estimable value. The Duke of Westminster, for instance, owns most of Oxford Street, Mayfair and Belgravia. His property holdings are guessed to be worth about £4,000 million. Apart from affluent individuals and families, there are important opulent corporations such as the universities of Oxford and Cambridge. These have immense fixed assets in town and country at their disposal. Their poorer sisters, the universities in Bradford, Birmingham, Stirling or Swansea, to name but a few, own nothing of the sort. Naturally, Oxbridge preserves strict silence on its property.

Ever since Margaret Thatcher's Conservative Government came to office in May 1979, the upper social strata have begun again to display serene self-confidence. Wealth and luxury have again become possible to an extent which seemed impossible in the wake of post-war social reforms. The dominating idea of the time had been that the world of the prosperous and the privileged had perished with World War II.

BRIDESHEAD REVISITED AND *A DANCE TO THE MUSIC OF TIME*: FAREWELL TO AN OLD AGE AND WELCOME TO ITS RETURN

English literature reflects this farewell to the old days. One of the most important novels in this context is *Brideshead Revisited* by Evelyn Waugh, published in 1945. The author was a bourgeois snob himself and admired traditional aristocracy. In his novel he provides an impressive picture of the sterility, decline, even decay of the world of the gentleman, whose glamour Waugh depicts as flaring up for a final time between the wars before its irretrievable extinction. In *Brideshead Revisited* the author invokes the decadent beauty and elegance of those marked by death. Waugh himself was an arch-reactionary politically, he quarrelled with his time and his values were derived from an idealized society of higher nobility. The book was serialized for television at great expense in 1980 by the respected writer and film director John Mortimer. Evelyn Waugh now belongs to the ten most widely read authors among university students of English literature. Waugh was born in 1903. He was the son of a publisher and literary critic, graduated from Oxford University and converted to catholicism in 1930. During World War II he served as an officer in the Middle East and Yugoslavia. Privately, he tried to lead the life of a gentleman of leisure. He was a member of several gentlemen's clubs (such as White's and Beefsteak). His arrogance towards a servant caused a scandal in Beefsteak once. His second marriage was to an aristocrat after which he moved to a substantial country mansion. Harbouring a distaste of all things modern, he collected Victorian paintings during a time when these enjoyed little esteem in the eyes of the general public. If the opinion of his contemporaries is anything to go by, Evelyn Waugh must have been both nasty and mis-anthropic. His development is quite symptomatic for the fascination exerted by Britain's aristocratically dominated society on many members of the country's intelligentsia.

Despite this (or perhaps because of it), this successful emulator of the ideal of the gentleman was able to write a satire on its obsolete conventions, which aptly characterized the spirit of the time and the development of society. *Brideshead Revisited* is a novel about the development of two young Oxford students. One of them, Sebastian Flyte, is descended from an ancient Catholic family of noble lineage, the second son of the Marquis of Marchmain. In Oxford, he moves in the circle of his Etonian friends between exquisite luncheons with champagne and lapwing's eggs and visits to the botanical garden (because he suddenly feels like seeing ivy). He carries a huge teddy bear around with him, which he has baptized Aloysius. As a devout Catholic, he prays to St Antonius of Padova when he loses Aloysius one day. With his eccentricity and his moods Sebastian represents the prototype of the aristocratic gentleman, who regards the world as his private playground. He seems a bizarre mixture of inoffensive naivety and imperious arrogance.

The novel is written as the first person narrative of Charles Ryder, an untitled but wealthy friend of Sebastian's. His mother, spurred by the example of Florence Nightingale, died of exhaustion in Bosnia. His father, uninterested and cold towards his son, lives the secluded life of a private scholar with his butler Hayter in London, immersed in his studies of Etruscan and ancient Egyptian Art. Charles had experienced a 'lonely childhood. . . and the hard youth of an English upbringing'. It is through Sebastian that he gets to know a general sense of carefreeness, unrestrainedness and luxury. He feels like catching up 'a short span of happy childhood'. After their first encounter Sebastian tells him: 'Oh, Charles, how much you have got to learn still!' The aristocrat educates the 'commoner'; and the latter proves to be a willing student. This unknown new world appears as paradise to the narrator. Hence the first section of the novel is called *'Et in Arcadia Ego'* (I was in Arcadia, too).

The joy of discovery and irresponsibility characterize these early years. Charles Ryder gives up his Oxford studies, visits an art school in Paris and within a few years becomes a fairly successful landscape artist. He marries a woman, whom he does not love, and with her has children towards whom he is indifferent. He leads a boring life between varnishing days and foreign travel to enrich his paintings with new motifs.

The crucial point of the novel, however, is the fate of Sebastian. He blossoms prematurely during his Arcadian days in Oxford. His life seems to fade out in an unnatural transition between childhood and old age. He becomes an alcoholic, is told to leave the university before time and eventually lives in Morroco with a young German, who has defected from the foreign legion. Why this decline of Sebastian? Charles had noticed the suffering of his friend, for which there did not seem to be any reason, right from the beginning, as well as his own helplessness towards the situation: 'He was sick at heart somewhere, I did not know how, and I grieved for him, unable to help.' (E. Waugh, 1960, p. 144.) Sebastian suffers particularly within his family whose desparate attempts at closeness generate demoralization. He keeps emphasizing how 'sweet and charming' his mother is, and yet her gentle pressure becomes virtually unbearable. Sebastian cannot identify himself with his family. However, by not rebelling he becomes a complete victim. He rejects his world passively without breaking with it; hence he is broken by it. When Sebastian shows Charles the splendid Brideshead estate for the first time, he explains 'this is where my family lives'. Charles perceives a certain coldness in this phrase: Sebastian did not say 'this is my home'.

The entire novel is permeated by the 'whisper of doom'. The story terminates with the outbreak of World War II. This real historic catastrophe adds a wider dimension to the literary illustration of individual disintegration. The English nobility, although alive, has outlived itself in historical terms. Hence they may adversely affect anything which comes in close contact with them. One of the novel's minor characters is Anthony Blanche, a homosexual dandy from a distinguished family and a friend of Sebastian's. He points out to Charles that the sweetness and charm of the Flyte family are over-refined expressions of a social class marked by death:

I took you out to dinner to warn you of charm. I warned you expressly and in great detail of the Flyte family. Charm is the great English blight. It does not exist outside these damp islands. It spots and kills anything it touches. It kills Love; it kills Art; I greatly fear, my dear Charles, it has killed *you*.   (E. Waugh, 1960, p. 301.)

Lady Marchmain, Sebastian's mother, is one of the most resolute advocates of the old order and a master of charm. When Sebastian learns of her death while in Morocco, he utters about her: 'Poor Mummy. She really was a femme fatale, wasn't she? She killed at a touch.' (E. Waugh, 1960, p. 238.) The word charm contains a fateful double-meaning, radiating amiability and attracting temptation. The latter may cast a spell over people, as it did with Charles, the commoner, who becomes victim.

It is quite revealing that the novel displays open hostility towards the working class. The world outlined in *Brideshead Revisited* focusses incestuously on itself. The labour movement comes into the course of action only once. And this was *the* historic moment when their voice could not be ignored: the General Strike in May 1926, the only general strike in the history of the British labour movement. Its defeat caused not only a swing to the right within the unions, but also a general demoralization of working people. This show-down of strength happened too early, was too disorganized and found too little support to shift the social balance of power.

Charles Ryder travelled from Paris to London out of a patriotic sense of duty to join the anti-strike militias who fought against potential rioters. Ever since the 1917 Russian Revolution the vision of an impending domestic revolution had haunted the aristocratic and middle classes. In London Charles Ryder remains fairly ineffective, however. He comes together with a group of martially-minded sons of bourgeois families who meet in the gentlemanly Bratt's Club. They equip themselves with truncheons to guard milk transports daily. Charles participates only once in a confrontation with young dock workers in London's East End. However, a revolution was nowhere in sight. After their service to the nation, these self-appointed cadets happily returned to the club: 'Next day the General Strike was called off and the country everywhere, except in the coal-fields, returned to normal. It was as though a beast long fabled for its ferocity had emerged for an hour, scented danger, and shrunk back to its lair. It had not been worth leaving Paris.' (E. Waugh, 1960, p. 230.)

It is less amazing that the class prejudices and snobbery presented here actually existed, than that they continue to exist today. Evelyn Waugh published a revised version of *Brideshead Revisited* in 1959, in which he deleted some of the more 'decadent' scenes. In his foreword to this edition, Evelyn Waugh comments with some astonishment that the world he portrayed still prevails: 'And the English aristocracy has maintained its identity to a degree that then (N.B. 1945) seemed impossible. . . Much of this book therefore is a panegyric preached over an empty coffin.' (E. Waugh, 1960, p. 10, preface.) Did Evelyn Waugh really misunderstand his own satire and see it as a eulogy? It is significant that even today the novel carries an enormous nostalgic appeal to many readers.

It seems to me that most English writers still succumb to the fascination of the old order. They have contributed to the interpretation of questionable conditions which sees them as being natural and positive. One of the most representative documents viewing society as a playground of power and wealth is Anthony Powell's twelve volume cycle *A Dance to the Music of Time*. Powell was born in 1905, the son of an officer, receiving his education at Eton and at the reputable Balliol College of Oxford University. He married into the aristocratic Pakenham family. Anthony Powell worked on *A Dance to the Music of Time* over the course of twenty-five years from the beginning of the 1950s to the mid 1970s. The twelve books contain an impressive panorama of people and events, ranging from public school education during the 1920s to the hunger marches during the Great Depression; from the spread of marxism on the periphery of the Communist Party to the French popular front under Léon Blum in the 1930s; from the Spanish Civil War and World War II to the re-formation of society after the war to McCarthyism, Hollywood, the Cold War and even the hippy sub-culture of the closing 1960s. The range of motifs is monumental but as for his literary medium, this was reduced to a single one: conversation. The entire cycle consists of an endless round of table-talk, discussions and, above all, parties and receptions. The reader never learns about current affairs directly from the narrator, but almost exclusively through conversation among the main characters.

This formal principle of the prose typifies the author's philosophy of life: events are secondary outcomes of people's struggles and aspirations. Powell's primary interest is in people's aspirations, desires and dreams. He presumes that people act according to three main ulterior motives: power, money, sexuality. History is hence reduced to a power struggle among individuals, reminiscent of the Italian princes during the Renaissance. Interestingly, Venice is the only foreign venue. The title, *A Dance to the Music of Time*, is programmatic: as is said at one point, people move in a perpetual 'ritual dance'. Power, money and sexuality represent the driving forces behind this dance. The social code of conduct regulates behaviour necessarily so that the resulting conflicts are dealt with in an orderly fashion. Powell's philosophy recalls the medieval principle *semper idem* (i.e. always the same). The cycle terminates with a long quotation from *The Anatomy of Melancholy* by Richard Burton published in 1621, in which a series of individual concepts from all areas of life are merely listed. Reality appears to be understood as the unstructured co-existence of an inextricable multitude of 'things', with the 'familiar' recurring perpetually.

Powell outlines his world from the perspective of the upper classes. The lower classes are represented by some left-leaning intellectuals, who have contacts with these circles. These committed individuals are represented negatively throughout. The leading figure in the cycle is Kenneth Widmerpool. Son of a not-very-rich fertilizer manufacturer, he is depicted as the archetype of a modern monster. He was educated at the same public school as the writer (Eton) and was a power-hungry careerist right from the beginning. A slimy opportunist among the powerful, he is full of intrigues and even after his rise remains pompous and petty. Widmerpool is clearly a sado-masochist who draws satisfaction from every humiliation and strength from every defeat. The type of person who gets everything he wants.

To Powell, he symbolizes the typical careerist from the gutter, who rises to the top in the wake of social upheavals. During the 1930s, Widmerpool supported the appeasement policies towards Hitler, then he served as a major behind the lines in the war, only to be subsequently elected as a Labour Member of Parliament. Showing communist sympathies, he entertains clandestine connections with the Soviet Union which are never uncovered. In old age, he leads a religious sect and publicly defends both the hippy sub-culture and the anti-authoritarian movement. The rise of Widmerpool historically reflects the Labour Party's accession to political power, which Powell interprets as the result of the opportunism of individuals who have their eyes set on penetrating the establishment. To Powell, politics has nothing to do with power struggles among social classes, but becomes a ritual of struggles between individual gladiators. His sympathies lie quite clearly with the upper classes.

Another character, Lord Warminster, also has communist sympathies. However, he is descended from the nobility. By contrast with Widmerpool's activities, his dealings are portrayed as the mere moods of an eccentric. As is emphasized several times, old family bonds prove stronger than new loyalties—be they marital or political. In *A Dance to the Music of Time* English society comes across as a collection of innumerable introverted cliques. Literary cliques and gentlemen's clubs are a visible expression of a deep contradiction within the nation: on the one hand there is considerable national cohesion and social tranquillity, but on the other hand one finds glaring divisions between social classes. The world described by English literature virtually ignores the working class, as if they were living on a different planet.

Some British literary critics have thought Anthony Powell's contribution to be of comparable importance to that of James Joyce and Marcel Proust. Some claim *A Dance to the Music of Time* to be the best prose work of post-war English literature.

CHAPTER TWO

The poor
and the
myth of the affluent society

REFORMING GOVERNMENTS AND
DISAPPOINTMENTS SINCE 1945

The extremes of poverty and wealth in our Western
European societies are largely invisible. In the middle of
London, for example, there are even today numerous
shelters for the homeless and shabby blocks of flats which
are, in many instances, unknown even to people in the
immediate neighbourhood. Although only a few streets
apart, people belonging to different social groups or classes
never move in the same social circles. In addition, housing
for the poor often creates a false impression of orderliness.
Misery may be hidden from the outside, but inside it is
often expressed in brutality and destruction. Long filthy
corridors, the smell of urine, windows sealed off with
wooden boards, steel doors replacing the ordinary wooden
entrance door: these are just some examples of what may
be found behind the façades of tower blocks which on
the surface seem well looked after. Dehumanization
through poverty represents a burden of human debt in
our societies. Individuals or social groups are doubly
victimized by society: firstly, by being cut off from the
mainstream of society and, secondly, by being stigmatized
as 'anti-social elements'.

The juxtaposition of grinding poverty and great wealth
is a symptom of a society founded on power. The history

of British society since World War II is a history of frustrated reforms. It begins with the Labour landslide in the 1945 general election and the high hopes for a radical transformation of society which this election victory carried in its wake. In 1950, some Labour politicians thought not only had the old, class-ridden society been overcome forever, but also that the introduction of a new, just, socialist society was unstoppable. Today, in the 1980s, British public opinion is dominated by scepticism and pessimism. One of the most profound disappointments of the four post-war decades is the experience that society is still closed, despite working class access to schools and universities, council housing, the National Health Service, the overall strengthening of the Labour movement and the increased legal security it enjoys. The promised emancipation of the lower classes has not happened. On the contrary, misery and unemployment are increasingly paralyzing the working classes. At the same time, the British bourgeoisie appears to have never had it so good since 1945. Their ideas dominate. Since the 1981 foundation of the new Social Democratic Party, SDP, it looks as if the British middle classes may seize a historic initiative on a party political level as well.

After World War II, the Labour Party was able for the first time in history to form a majority government on its own. The 1945–1951 Labour Government created the National Health Service and nationalized some key industries such as coal and the railways. Quite rightly, the Labour Party today looks back on this first great period of reforming government with pride. During the first six post-war years, the foundations of the so-called 'mixed economy' were laid, foundations which (once laid) have been supported by both Labour and Conservative governments until 1979. Although during the late 1940s these new foundations meant a courageous break with an obsolete system, they gradually evolved into an inflexible machinery, the weaknesses of which have been laid particularly at the door of the Labour Party. The 1964–

1970 Labour Government under Prime Minister Harold Wilson was soundly beaten at the polls in June 1970. Harold Wilson began his premiership with the pledge to revitalize the reforming impulses of the post war period as well as to build a modern society. He announced fundamental reforms under the motto 'the white heat of technology': technological renewal was also meant to transform society socially. By contrast with today, Britain then was in a national mood of reform. For although decolonization had not been carried out entirely without social upheaval (the Mau-Mau uprising in Kenya, for instance, or the Suez aggression against Nasser's Egypt), it was brought to peaceful completion through the creation of the Commonwealth. The British Empire had ceased to exist. Great Britain was getting ready to assume a place in the world community which was in accordance with, as well as abreast of, the times. The third (and so far last) phase of post-war Labour Government from 1974–1979 did not command a sufficient majority in the House of Commons. The 1976 loan from the International Monetary Fund (IMF) obliged Prime Minister James Callaghan to undertake a series of drastic economies in the public sector as well as to pursue a restrictive incomes policy. This deepened the crisis of trust between the labour movement and the Labour Party. James Callaghan lost the 1979 general election after a wave of strikes during the 1978 'winter of discontent'. The Labour Party then obtained their lowest share of the vote since 1945. In the 1983 general election, yet a further serious erosion in the Labour vote took place.

The course of events during the three post-war periods of Conservative Government shows striking similarities with the fate of the Labour Party. The first phase from 1951–1964 was a period of stability and undisputed social consensus. The 1970–1974 Conservative Government under Edward Heath, however, followed a rather more confrontationist approach vis-à-vis the labour movement and suffered several defeats. The failure of this period led to a sharp shift to the right within the Conservative Party, which resulted in the election of Margaret Thatcher as leader of the Conservative Party in 1975. The third, still continuing phase of Conservative Government began in 1979. As Prime Minister, Margaret Thatcher abruptly dismissed the policies of consensus which had characterized the governments of her post-war predecessors. In rejecting this British post-war consensus, she particularly broke with the important principle (which had been tacitly accepted by all parties), whereby one of the main tasks of government was a reduction of social differences and a more just distribution of wealth. Government policy under Margaret Thatcher is almost exclusively geared towards economic reconstruction. Goals of social reform have completely disappeared from the vocabulary of Conservative politicians and, significantly, from the vocabulary of the media as well. In her speeches, Margaret Thatcher constantly reiterates only one goal of her government's policies: the creation of 'an economy of free enterprise, the survival of which will depend on its capability to satisfy the needs and wishes of its customers'. The Conservative Government has already vigorously pursued a very comprehensive programme of privatization and is poised to push back the mixed economy on all fronts, even in areas dominated by public services, such as energy, transport, telecommunications, the Post Office, the National Health Service. A considerable number of highly profitable public companies have already been sold off to the private sector, such as Amersham, Britoil, Cable and Wireless, British Telecom. Further huge flotations are planned, for example British Gas, British Airways, the British Airports Authority, or even selected regional water authorities. Selling the lucrative parts of British Leyland, the coal industry or the engineering workshops of British Rail, is kept under constant review and appears underpinned by drastic job losses. Privatizing popular public institutions, like the Ordnance Survey of Great Britain or BBC Radios One and Two, is being discussed. Privatization policies look set to encroach upon every sector of society.

Such a radical return to the principle of the privately run economy was possible only because public debate had blamed previous reforming policies for economic decline. The post-war political aims of the Conservatives had been to make Britain a nation composed of small capitalists; the post-war programmes of the Labour Party had been to secure full employment and prosperity for all. Both parties have failed. Failure of these policies led to a disorientation and disillusion in public thinking, paving the way to the general opinion that only the private entrepreneur is capable of giving guidance to the economy. One consequence is the recent enormous rise in poverty, without parallel since World War II.

Several million unemployed people means several million socially degraded people. In 1982, the Labour Party estimated the number of people living at or below the poverty line to be nine million (1986 estimates by Frank Field MP, based on parliamentary answers, go up to thirteen million (The *Guardian*, 12 May 1986)). The United Kingdom possesses a population of 56 million, she still represents one of the strongest industrial nations in the world and has enormous resources. Why does the urge to increase wealth generate increased poverty? Impoverishment on one side and continuation of the class differences on the other are no secret. British media regularly report on these matters; even conservative papers talk about 'classes' and the 'class society'. Competent government departments publish surveys on poverty, welfare organizations deplore obvious grievances, and numerous publications by concerned individuals have collected plenty of material relating to the 'why?' and 'how?' of poverty. Despite all this effort, the question of poverty is not really topical in public debate. Poverty is as invisible today as it was in the nineteenth century. Then, many people derived their knowledge on matters of poverty primarily from stories and novels by poets and writers such as Charles Dickens. It appears unbelievable to us today how wealthy people at that time not just ignored poverty, but furthermore pushed it from their minds. When in the nineteenth century big cholera epidemics threatened to encroach upon parts of London previously unaffected, some social conditions became known, but were greeted with widespread scepticism. It was unimaginable to the wealthy around 1900 that an official investigation had produced evidence that some poor people had absolutely no idea what furniture was for. They had to be taught by means of illustrations the functions of wardrobes and chests of drawers, and how they may be best arranged in a dwelling.

POORHOUSES: PAST AND PRESENT

One of the most important original sources of the situation of the poor in nineteenth century London is the monumental work of journalist Henry Mayhew. From 1848 onwards, he systematically collected material on the poor, their way of life in general and their working lives in particular. Apart from its statistical content and apart from the parliamentary debates it deals with, his four-volume *London Labour and the London Poor* (1851) contains numerous life histories in the words of poor people themselves. They were mostly people who tried to survive in the British capital by occasional employment, theft, begging or prostitution. The picture of misery and poverty generated by the self-portraits of this army of declassed people is fairly familiar to today's readers as a result of the extensive documentation of the industrial revolution. The parallels to today's situation are quite frightening. In one chapter of his book, Henry Mayhew deals in detail with conditions in the so-called 'low lodging houses'. His report is illustrated by the life histories of a pickpocket, a prostitute and a beggar. The prostitute is an orphan and only sixteen years old. She was sent to take up some sort of employment at the age of ten and ran away after continuous ill-treatment. Looking for accommodation, she entered a lodging house, where she made friends with a fifteen-year-old pickpocket, who unfortunately was soon sent to prison. Prostitution remained her last chance of survival. This life of 'freedom' is so gruelling and meaningless to her that she prefers to go to prison, too:

I stole a piece of beef from a butcher. I did it to get into prison. I was sick of the life I was leading, and didn't know how to get out of it. I had a month for stealing. When I got out I passed two days and a night in the streets doing nothing wrong, and then went and threatened to break Messrs. ——— windows again. I did that to get into prison again; for when I lay quiet of a night in prison, I thought things over, and considered what a shocking life I was leading, and how my health might be ruined completely, and I thought I would stick to prison rather than go back to such a life. I got six months for threatening. When I got out I broke a lamp next morning for the same purpose, and had a fortnight.   (Mayhew, 1851, p. 413.)

A life of poverty without hope of improvement in one's circumstances makes many adolescents even today tired of life before their life has really begun. The extensive possibilities of our time are still simply non-existent for many people. In one and the same society there are so many different worlds as if they were separated by the centuries. For the needy, history has stagnated. Techno-logical and social progress possess virtually no meaning for them. Unchanged throughout the centuries, life is only about sheer physical survival. They have no reserves to protect themselves against the hardships of society. Under such circumstances, even the smallest personal loss may turn into a personal catastrophe. Against this background, life in prison seems more human to some of them than life outside. The following newspaper report is not untypical. On 18 April 1980, the *Daily Telegraph* reported that fifty-seven-year-old Dennis Brown, unemployed and with-out permanent address, had purposely broken a window pane of a public building and that he had given the follow-ing declaration at the magistrate's court: 'When I am released from prison, I shall continue to break window panes, so that I shall be back in prison. I want to stay in prison, because I am looked after there. I am always sent to overnight shelters, but one is only allowed to stay there for a fortnight. Then I shall have to go on the street again.' The magistrate's judge showed some mercy and sentenced him to three weeks imprisonment for the broken window pane.

The number of homeless people in Great Britain is estimated to be 150,000. In the cities, tramps belong once again to the familiar street picture. A large, shapeless coat, matted hair and worn-out, badly-fitting shoes typify the older tramps. The younger ones are not quite as easy to make out. Their inner resistance is not yet broken, and the sub-cultural milieus of the punks, rockers and skin-heads offer a possible identity outside the broad pattern of 'the successful' and 'the failed'. These sub-cultures, how-ever, have not arisen from disgust at the wealthy society, but represent expressions of deprivation and hopelessness. 'We are the flowers of the dustbin', a bitter metaphor in a song by the punk group *Sex Pistols*. The picture of the philosophical vagrant or the drunken tramp has nothing to do with the reality of most homeless people, young or old. Although some city or country tramps seek comfort in alcohol, only about 8 per cent of homeless people are actually alcoholics, and their alcoholism is mostly conse-quence, rather than cause, of their situation.

Every day, teenagers arrive in London from all parts of the country and even abroad. They have with them perhaps a few pounds in their pockets, a few personal belongings and great expectations. The old myth still surrounds the capital. Everything in the metropolis is different, as if all laws applicable to the rest of society were here no longer in force. Somehow one might be able to make it in London, find a room, job, friends. Lead an independent life. Many do not even have an address. They hitch-hike to the outskirts of London, ask around and gradually reach the city centre. Familiar street names begin to appear, known to them from school or from stories.

Then they stand in front of Piccadilly Circus in Soho and they do not know any further. They have arrived right in the heart of London, but the city itself remains closed to them. Where to go? The first great disillusionment is the experience of loneliness in big city life: nowhere to go; expected nowhere; nowhere to have a rest; while all other people seem busy and purposeful. Welfare organizations and advice bureaux are then the last resort. But these can only show a way which will lead to social degradation. They pass on addresses of cheap accommodation and refer to the possibility of occasional employment in hotels or warehouses. The earnings are insufficient to rent a room of one's own and it usually does not take long until this sort of life leads to resignation. One gradually becomes a prisoner of a certain milieu which is separated from the rest of society by an invisible line of demarcation. The society of our time continues to cast aside the *Lumpen-proletariat*, the class of the dispossessed, which vegetates quite literally in the chinks and cracks of our civilization.

There is a precise English expression which may be used not only to refer to the country and city tramps them-selves but also to describe their state of affairs: *down and out*. Down-and-outs vegetate miserably alongside sewers, bridges, railway arches, rubbish tips. The *Daily Telegraph* of 27 March 1981 reported that sixty-six-year-old Fred Taylor had been living in wooden boxes at the Eston rubbish tip (Cleveland) for years. Before that he had lived in a drainpipe and his address at social security was report-ed to have been: Drainpipe No 1, Eston tip. Even rubbish containers seem to provide a relatively quiet place of refuge for some down-and-outs, although these can be dangerous. In this context, *The Guardian* reported on 16 April 1981:

Rude awakening saves tramp
A TRAMP narrowly escaped being mangled to death in a refuse crushing machine after sleeping the night in a giant bin at a shopping centre in Kettering, Northants. As the bin was to be tipped into the

council crusher yesterday morning one of the dustmen noticed an arm sticking out. After being dragged out the tramp left without saying a word.

Why do many tramps apparently prefer to spend the night outside than in the numerous poorhouses, welfare homes or other emergency accommodation? Everywhere in the cities and in the country there are council quarters, homes run by the Salvation Army or by other welfare organizations as well as private overnight accommodation. These houses range from huge, converted, inner-city blocks of flats to run-down former army barracks and empty one-family homes utilized by the council for emergency accommodation. Would it not be better to have some sort of roof over one's head or to sleep in a real bed at night? The answer to this question is both simple and discouraging: in the quarters mentioned above, dirt, degradation and communal depression await the homeless person. To many homeless people, this kind of restraint is less tolerable than the hopelessness of the street. These temporary shelters do much to make homeless people conscious of being stigmatized as the down-and-outs of society. Permanent residence in temporary quarters means losing touch completely with the rest of society.

In his book on the London poor of the nineteenth century, Henry Mayhew also added some remarks concerning the condition of the poorhouses of the time, most of which were owned privately. Mayhew traced the earnings of the owners and concluded that the accumulation of pennies secured enormous extra income. Even today, there still exists privately owned emergency accommodation, which is recognized as night shelter by the social security. A person in need receives a coupon for overnight accommodation from social security which entitles him or her to use a private night shelter. The owner of this accommodation will then be reimbursed for this service upon return of the coupon. When property owners convert houses to night shelters, then this usually means that this particular property is in too poor a condition to be offered for sale or rent on the open market. Even poverty can become a profitable business in a society containing so many poor people. Where there is great need even ruins may serve as a source of personal gain. According to Henry Mayhew, poorhouses were hotbeds of crime, full of youth learning the art of survival from the old. Brawling made the atmosphere dangerous for anybody not familiar with the rules of fist fighting. By contrast with today's night shelters, there was no separation of the sexes either. Hence, they often assumed the functions of a brothel as well. Furthermore, Mayhew's interviewees invariably complained about beds and sanitary facilities, both incredibly dirty, clogged with filth. The term 'sanitary facilities' is probably sheer euphemism anyway. Foul smells penetrated the vermin-ridden rooms. One of Henry Mayhew's sources reported:

These beds were made—as all the low lodging-house beds are—of the worst cotton flocks stuffed in coarse, strong canvas. There is a pair of sheets, a blanket and a rug. I have known the bedding to be unchanged for three months; but that is not general. The beds are an average size. Dirt is the rule with them, and cleanliness the exception. They are all infested with vermin. . . In some houses in the summer you can hardly place your finger on a part of the wall free from bugs. I have scraped them off by handfulls.

(Mayhew, 1851, pp. 408–9.)

Also, the smell of the residents' foul breath was intolerable and worsened by inadequate ventilation. In some of the mixed dormitories, there was just a bucket for people to relieve themselves.

DOWN AND OUT IN LONDON

Nearly eighty years after Mayhew's investigations, George Orwell wrote his book *Down and Out in Paris and London* (1933) about the life of city tramps. The appalling circumstances described by Mayhew had undergone fundamental change only in a very few particulars. By 1933, men and women were not allowed to stay in the same room or dormitory and care for the poor lay in the hands of welfare organizations. Also, there was a new type of night shelter: quarters administered by the council, which the tramps called 'spikes'. Orwell describes an overnight stay in such a 'spike'. Just before six o'clock tramps crowd the entrance of this home, which is shut during the day. Then, everyone is admitted and all personal details taken down; name, profession, age, last overnight shelter. Communal washing follows thereafter. Orwell writes: 'The scene in the bathroom was extraordinarily repulsive. Fifty dirty, stark-naked men elbowing each other in a room twenty feet square, with only two bath-tubs and two slimy roller towels between them all.' (Orwell, 1933, p. 145.) They must hand in their clothes for a grey nightgown. After a meal consisting of bread and margarine as well as a mug of bitter cocoa, they are allocated (in twos) a tiny room in which to sleep. This room is locked from the outside at about seven p.m. and will only be opened again at eight a.m. As in prison, these cells contain barred windows and doors with peepholes. Both 'residents' are given six blankets and one chamber-pot. There are no beds. The only source of heat comes from a hot water pipe on the wall. The cell is so tiny that the two people are inevitably going to roll against each other while asleep; they will be able to feel each other's breath in their faces. The next morning everybody has to undergo a brief check-up which, however, does not serve the purpose of disease detection and medical care in general, but merely of diagnosing the presence or absence of smallpox. Orwell recalls:

Naked and shivering, we lined up in the passage. You cannot conceive what ruinous, degenerate curs we looked, standing there in the merciless morning light. A tramp's clothes are bad, but they conceal far worse things: to see him as he really is, unmitigated, you must see him naked. Flat feet, pot bellies, hollow chests, sagging muscles—

every kind of physical rottenness was there. Nearly everyone was under-nourished, and some clearly diseased; two men were wearing trusses, and as for the old mummy-like creature of seventy-five, one wondered how he could possible make his daily march. Looking at our faces, unshaven and creased from the sleepless night, you would have thought that all of us were recovering from a week on the drink.

(Orwell, 1933, pp. 147–8.)

Orwell had these experiences around 1930 during the time of the Depression. Fifty years later BBC reporter Tony Wilkinson spent four weeks among the tramps of London. He queues with them in front of job centres at four o'clock in the morning, sleeps in night shelters run by the Salvation Army and in those run by social security, stays some nights in house entrances or under bridges by the Thames, learns the tricks of the trade from tramps, especially how to 'organize' something to eat. One of the best temporary jobs is apparently offered by the great luxury hotels in Mayfair. These employ casual labour for the kitchen just for the day. To many job-seekers, the numerous hotels and restaurants represent the last resort. Conversely, to the hotel trade this source of cheap labour is sometimes the condition of continued existence. There is no sector of the economy where there are so few industrial agreements or union representations as in the hotel trade. This sector would not be able to offer the luxury of service and attendance at present prices if it were not for the army of job seekers willing to work the whole day for a mere pittance, cleaning pots and pans as well as washing vegetables. Tony Wilkinson asked himself what the distinguished guests of Mayfair or Claridge's would think if they knew that he had just been hired from the street along with others in order to prepare food for the dining hall? He, who could have been a real tramp bearing some infectious disease; he, who had spent the night before in a dirty gateway; he, who was not even asked to wash before starting to work?

Many of the day labourers in the great hotels are also

permanent guests in the night shelters in the city centre. Their wages are not sufficient to rent a room privately, especially not in the suburbs as the bus or underground fares would use up most of their earnings. Some of the big night shelters in the city like Bruce House, situated in the pleasant tourist quarter Covent Garden, are even listed buildings. There are huge, residential blocks of flats, which look quite ordinary from the outside. The visitor would hardly be able to guess what is behind this neutral façade, and perhaps even contemplates with agreeable surprise flats for ordinary people within easy reach of the expensive little boutiques, restaurants as well as opera and theatre. The architecture of our cities seems to reveal very little about the social structure or stratification of people living in them. Behind the façade of former middle class buildings of the nineteenth century may reside an inter-locking maze of run-down one-room flats, even in parts of London like Kensington or Notting Hill. On the other hand, the former mews, which used to be the place of residence for servants, have often been converted into small luxury homes. It seems as if everybody practises the art of pretence. The class-ridden society has long since responded to its critics by cannily hiding its visible symbols. These symbols continue to exist, however, but understanding them has become more difficult.

In 1979, the social scientist Professor Peter Townsend published his monumental study *Poverty in the United Kingdom* which has already become a classical work on the economic circumstances of the lower strata of British society. Peter Townsend concludes in his study that the introduction of social security has not fundamentally changed the problem of poverty. On the contrary, in public opinion measures such as these led to an institution-alized view of the needs of income in modern British society, a view which is narrow and mean. The concept of 'redistribution of wealth' was given a restrictive meaning.

There is the English expression 'beggars can't be choosers'. The saying is meant as a repudiation of unjust claims. It could also be taken as a hint, however, that there is a basic deficit in the humanist principles of our societies, whereby certain groups of people are not even theoretically given the same rights as the well-to-do. The problem of poverty is not just a problem of improving our welfare institutions. A fundamental change will only occur when society ceases to cast aside what it regards as 'excess people', i.e. if society changes its functioning to the extent that individual failures are no longer punished by banning to a 'penal colony for anti-socials'.

Journalist Tony Wilkinson published his experiences (which he had had in 1980) in a book which he called *Down and Out* in accordance with George Orwell. What is striking in his report is not so much the facts he relates but his description of the tramps' way of life in the midst of a world so familiar to us. Every day, they go from station to station in the British capital, following a path which resembles the tourist sightseeing route: Westminster, Embankment, Charing Cross, Covent Garden, Tower Bridge, King's Cross, Camden Town and Hampstead Heath—all famous names which have become stations of misery for the tramps. Their destinations are: the mobile kitchens of the welfare organizations which distribute soup at certain places; the weekly markets, which offer partly spoiled fruit; supermarkets, in the dustbins of which perhaps semi-rotten meat may be found; social security offices and, for some, new night shelters, because they have been ordered to stay away from other homes. Tramps mostly move in the midst of the world shared by the rest of society and yet they are exiled from it. Quite contrary to their anarchic existence, their way of life is strictly regimented. All homes have exact opening and closing times, the police only allow certain hours for resting in public places, everywhere there are rules, regulations, coupons. The latter have to be applied for again and again if a particular right is not to be lost. There is a military regime in night shelters, no matter whether these are privately or publicly run. Tony Wilkinson describes his first night in Bruce House, the aforementioned listed building in Covent Garden serving as a dosshouse (*see* figure 6). At 10.30 p.m. he queues with thirty other men in front of a staircase leading to the cells where they would sleep. The staircase is barred with an iron grating. People wait to be allocated cells, after they had already had to wait for some time at the entrance to Bruce House:

I heard the iron gate being unlocked. I felt like a prisoner conspiring with my guards, someone consenting to be locked up. The line began to move forward past a man in casual clothes who stood sentry by the gate. Several men ahead of me showed him their bed tickets as they passed, but always from a distance, as a token gesture. He nodded, but stopped no one. I passed by, too, a newcomer, a person worth checking, but he did not examine my ticket. I tried to work out in my own mind what function the gate was intended to serve. If it was to make sure that only those with tickets had been allowed up, why had there been no scrutiny? And if there was no scrutiny, why have gates at all? It seemed to be a meaningless ritual. But perhaps it had another purpose—to keep us in our place. I felt humiliated to have to queue to go to bed. I had been kept waiting, I had been obliged to pass through a barrier, I had been noted by Authority. Perhaps that was the whole point.

My cubicle was a tiny open-topped cell on the second floor, one of more than a hundred in a maze of corridors and fire doors. The side-walls were painted cream and seemed to be made of metal. The bed was a three-inch mattress on a plywood base, the sheets newly washed but grey with the sweat of years. There were two blankets, and there seemed to be no heating.

I could see the urine in the corridor outside, and I wondered where the lavatories were. I had seen only one on my floor. It was by the stairs, and a long walk off.　　　(Wilkinson, 1981, pp. 79–80.)

A prison atmosphere and dirt are still the dominating hallmarks of an overnight asylum. Since the 1960s, regular investigations on the fate and social origins of homeless people have been carried out in Great Britain. The Department of the Environment is responsible for these studies. Although these studies present their statistical analyses extremely cautiously by avoiding any question about general social causes, they still contain important hints as to how the social decline of homeless people occurs. The 1981 ministerial study *Single and Homeless* clearly showed that the stereotype of the aged city tramp is thoroughly inadequate. Firstly, it is stated that the proprotion of young people is high. A young woman says: 'We're not dossers, but we're people, who just have not got anywhere to go. Most young people who are homeless—either they do not get on with their parents or their marriage breaks up.' (Department of the Environment, HMSO, 1981, p. 21.) Secondly, the majority of homeless people possesses only minimal education. Surprisingly many, however, have successfully completed a vocational training: clerical assistant, bricklayer, factory worker, businessman. These are usually ordinary working people who have lost their employment through private difficulties, which have initiated the long spiral of decline. The DoE study under-lines especially the fact that a substantial number of homeless people are vocationally trained. In this world of homelessness, stability is difficult to preserve. Homeless people experience increased restlessness, which the DoE study calls 'mobility'; places of employment and residence are changed ever more frequently. How many of them succeed in breaking this vicious circle? Due to their increasing restlessness how many are caught up in an ever quicker and deeper maelstrom until they are irreversibly *down and out*?

CHANGE OF SELF-IMAGE

Today in the 1980s, poverty is again an actual and acute structural problem of British society. Unemployment figures totalling several million people can hardly be explained as a peripheral phenomenon due to individuals' inadequacies. It took a long time before it was officially admitted that Great Britain is not a society of generally widespread wealth as propagated by the 1960s slogan of

the 'affluent society'. This grudging admission sheds light
on the change of self-image which Great Britain has
undergone since the end of World War II.

The myth of the affluent society dominated public
perceptions unbrokenly throughout the 1950s. The
Labour Party congratulated itself on the successful introduction of welfare measures and institutions, and the
Conservatives accepted the welfare state as the up-to-date
expression of the capitalist economy which seemed to be
reconcilable with the latter's interests. It was a time of
prosperity and ascent, but also of social blindness. The years
of deprivation due to the war appeared to be over and the
new social formula promised to ban unemployment and
economic crises forever. 'You never had it so good' was
Prime Minister Harold Macmillan's main slogan for the
1959 general election. It looked as if the re-distribution of
wealth had been achieved smoothly and peacefully. The
rosy revisionism of the Labour Party and the reformism of
the Conservative Party seemed to converge in a unique
consensus which has been given conceptual expression in
the English language: 'Butskellism', an amalgam of the
surnames of Conservative Cabinet Minister R.A. Butler and
Labour leader Hugh Gaitskell. At that time, further
concepts were created which dominated the vocabulary of
leading politicians until the late 1970s: 'postcapitalism',
'partnership', 'consensus politics', 'mixed economy', and,
of course, 'affluent society'. The ideology of the crisis-
free affluent society blinded so completely that during the
1950s almost no investigations concerning poverty were
conducted. One of the very few studies by Seebohm
Rowntree concluded in 1950 that British society contained
only 1 per cent poor people. Only few investigators or
thinkers doubted the results or the methodology of this
study. The few people who did so, like Peter Townsend,
who started on his life-long research work on the problem
of poverty at about that time, remained unheard for a
long time.

It was not until the 1960s that a critical rethink began.

Nevertheless, studies confirming the alleged affluence of the working class, like John H. Goldthorpe's *The affluent worker* (1968), continued to dominate public opinion, although public perception had already begun to shift markedly. The Conservative Party was thought of as has-been and, among youth, rebellion against the complacency of the older generation became noticeable. In 1965, Peter Townsend, together with Brian Abel-Smith, published his first pioneering investigation called *The Poor and the Poorest*. The results presented formed a complete contrast with official ideology. The authors showed that in 1953 already 7.8 per cent of the population were living in poverty and by 1960 this figure had increased to 14.2 per cent, i.e. 7.5 million people.

Of course, glossing over the existence of widespread poverty did not end with the publication of a sober social scientific analysis. The Labour Party attempted to rally people behind a new beginning under the motto of technological revolution. Labour furthermore fostered the illusion that all social problems could be solved by the 'modernization of the obsolete'. Although the problem of poverty was acknowledged to exist, it was rather understood as the problem of individuals caught up in a cycle of deprivation. A 1969 Home Office publication, when the Labour Government was still in power, designated the following stages in this vicious cycle: 'poor health—financial difficulties—children suffering under the implications of decline—consequent possible youth criminality—inability of children to adapt to the adult world—unstable marriages—emotional problems—poor health— and the cycle starts afresh'. Substantial progress may be detected in the fact that the individual tragedy lying behind impoverishment was officially reported in this way. This may have led to increased public awareness of the problem. However, the sort of interpretation outlined above contributed considerably to the view that the alleviation of poverty is primarily a problem of improving welfare organizations. This in turn was to be done by simplifying their bureaucracy and improving their funding as well as their functioning. The official ideology did not discuss poverty or unemployment as a question of *structural* faults within capitalist society; not then, nor to this day.

The new Conservative philosophy rather alleges the opposite: it is not structural faults within capitalist society which cause unemployment, but political deviation from the old principles of the privately run economy. According to this philosophy, the crisis of British society today is the result of thirty years of 'socialist mismanagement'. To the extent that a degree of nationalization and trade union participation in economic decision-making are equated with 'socialism', more comprehensive concepts of a real socialist transformation of society are banned or tabooed from public debate. There is generally a feeling within Great Britain that the functioning of society is in some ways paralyzed. The entrepreneur feels himself hindered by the practises of organized labour—it is felt that techno-logical change and diversification of products proceed too slowly since union agreements have to be secured first. There are rival institutions within the apparatus of the state, and when these institutions are dominated by rival political parties, decisions made by one institution may well be blocked by the other. For example, the Labour-led Greater London Council (GLC) introduced its cheap fares policy for London Transport (LT) in 1981. Conservative-led central Government introduced legislation to make these measures illegal. The House of Lords then ruled in a politically motivated judgement that the GLC did not possess the right to increase the London ratepayer's burden by the considerable reduction of fares. This curtail-ment of GLC policy was probably a prelude to the abolition of the Greater London Council and the other Metropolitan County Councils in April 1986. The Conservative Govern-ment's huge majority in Parliament clearly ignored the wishes of the people concerned by enacting the necessary legislation for doing so. Every Council concerned opposed the measure, and every opinion poll backed this opposition with decisive majorities.

THE POLITICS OF POVERTY

Britain's economic problems are nothing new; the nation's gradual economic decline from its one-time position as 'workshop of the world' may be traced back to the nineteenth century. The accumulation of vast wealth and political supremacy, however, have contributed to the masking of symptoms. Only after the dissolution of the Empire did it become apparent how little Great Britain was fit to stand up to free competition with her international rivals. But even if Britain's present economic problems are not new, her social crisis is. It seems as if the forces of capitalism and the forces of socialism have reached approximate parity for the first time. This probably gives Conservatives the feeling of having to mount a huge effort, now or never, in order to reverse this relative shift of power. Before becoming Prime Minister, Margaret Thatcher declared on the eve of the 1979 general election that 'this election probably represents the last chance to reverse this process'. Mrs Thatcher depicts this historic process differently, of course, by defining it as 'the increasing shift of the social balance in favour of the state and at the expense of the individual'. Significantly, this attack on the state is not directed against those institutions of the state such as the police, the armed forces or the judiciary, but against organizations of the state which are supposed to be controlled by 'socialists', such as social welfare and public services. According to the Conservative argument it is businessmen and entrepreneurs who are harrassed by the state. The 1979 and 1983 Conservative manifestos expressively envisaged the goal of a 'property-owning democracy', first formulated by Sir Anthony Eden (Conservative Prime Minister 1955–1957), in which every single individual controls some capital.

The Labour Party similarly sees its task as shifting the social balance, although in a different direction. The 1979

Labour manifesto said that what is at stake is to 'effect a fundamental and irreversible shift in the balance of social power and wealth in favour of working people and their families'. Since the Labour Party's swing to the left in the late 1970s and early 1980s, fundamental structural changes in British society are regarded as concrete tasks for a future Labour Government even at the highest levels of the party. For the first time since 1945, the British Left has composed the programme of an alternative economic strategy, which is largely supported by the unions, the Labour Party, the Communist Party and other groupings on the left. The House of Commons contains several members who possess quite clear conceptions on the problem of overcoming British class society. The young Labour MP Frank Field, Member for Birkenhead, who has been active in the areas of welfare and low pay for several years, interprets the question of poverty in his study *Inequality in Britain* as a structural problem of British society. He defines: 'Poverty is seen largely as a consequence of the current distribution of income and wealth in our society, and while particular individuals may escape from poverty by their own efforts, the structure of earnings and benefits ensures that other individuals will take their place.' (F. Field, 1981, p. 19.)

Hence, the possibility of individual social mobility has not changed the existence of rich and poor strata in society. In his quotation, Frank Field deliberately talks about income *and* wealth, because the discrepancies of income between the working and professional classes only vaguely hint at the real overall distribution of wealth. As far as the middle classes and the aristocracy are concerned, the salary is rarely the only source of income to secure a particular standard of living. Both social groups have accumulated wealth at their disposal, which in times of crisis may amount to a decisive reserve. If a worker, however, does not receive any wages, he or she is not normally able to maintain his or her standard of living. The average savings of a worker do not even equal two months' wages, and his or her furnishings do not usually contain valuable keepsakes which are readily convertible into money. The consequence of this nearly complete lack of financial reserves is that unemployment or individual difficulties like severe illnesses or marital problems may cause a marked social decline almost overnight.

Frank Field, former director of the Child Poverty Action Group, calculated that the number of poor people has doubled under Mrs Thatcher's premiership. Defining 'poor' as 'eligible for supplementary benefit', and basing his analysis on parliamentary answers, Frank Field observed the number of people dependent on social security to be 6.5 million in 1979, 10.6 million in February 1985 and estimated to be 13 million in May 1986 (The *Guardian*, 12 May 1986, p. 3).

David Donnison, chairman of the government commission on social security from 1975–1980, has for years visited needy people in council housing and dealt with their applications for support. He concluded that the human tragedy resulting from impoverishment is the social exclusion of the people affected from the communities in which they previously participated. In his book *The Politics of Poverty*, David Donnison quotes a section from the commission's report to Parliament which describes the human consequences of poverty:

To keep out of poverty [we said in our Report for 1978], people must have an income which enables them to participate in the life of the community. They must be able, for example, to keep themselves reasonably fed, and well enough dressed to maintain their self-respect and to attend interviews for jobs with confidence. Their homes must be reasonably warm; their children should not feel shamed by the quality of their clothing; the family must be able to visit relatives, and give them something on their birthdays and at Christmas time; they must be able to read newspapers, and retain their television sets and their membership of trade unions and churches. And they must be able to live in a way which ensures, so far as possible, that public officials, doctors, teachers, landlords and others treat them with the courtesy due to every member of the community. (Donnison, 1982, p. 8.)

Successful people still have difficulty imagining what poverty actually means. In interviews with the authors of poverty studies, there is frequent repeated questioning by disbelieving reporters. Furthermore, many leading articles in the big daily papers display open cynicism concerning questions of poverty. Ruling ideology relegates the issue of poverty to a problem pertaining to peripheral groupings of society, and treats poverty as a matter for welfare organizations only. Because the development of our society is both unequal and separate, poverty seems experiencable only to people directly affected by it. The various strata of society are virtually hermetically shut off from one another, so that the various ways of life remain mostly unknown to one another. On the one hand, there is a public consciousness created by the mass media, which seems to cover all areas transparently, on the other hand, however, we remain extremely isolated in our actual daily dealings. The functioning of our society had created an antagonism between private and public worlds, causing a complete lack of knowledge of other spheres of life. The extreme separation of the world of the rich from the world of the poor in Great Britain is still as deep as if nothing had changed since the nineteenth century. London in particular gives the impression of a bubbling metropolis which amuses itself in the midst of crisis and misery, rather like the Berlin of the 1920s. The most expensive luxury shops in Mayfair and Knightsbridge, the transactions of business connected with world trade in the City, an amazing abundance of film performances, theatre productions, concerts and exhibitions all invoke the picture of a golden epoch. Prince Philip does not understand why some people are dissatisfied. He declared: 'A few years ago everybody was saying "We must have more leisure—everybody's working too much". Now that everybody's got so much leisure—it may be involuntary but they've got it—they're complaining they're unemployed. People don't seem to be able to make up their minds what they want, do they?' (Prince Philip, *Daily Express*, 11 June 1981.)

Michael Heseltine, as Secretary of State for the Environment, paid a visit to hard-hit Liverpool after the inner-city riots of summer 1981. He interrupted his fact-finding mission in the deprived and run-down parts of Liverpool to return home for the weekend on the occasion of a big party given by his daughter Annabel who thereby made her formal entry into society. About 400 guests were invited and the total bill came to nearly £10,000. A spokesman replied to the question whether the Cabinet Minister could really spare the time during such a critical mission: 'I believe it goes without saying that Mr Heseltine should return home for such an important occasion.' The crisis of the British economy appears to affect only some strata of society, others seem obviously better off than ever before. To many, the age of closures, redundancies, bankruptcies brings new sources of wealth; the misfortune of one is the fortune of somebody else. The royal horse races at Ascot—since 1811 an annual meeting point for the upper circles—now rent out private lodges during the twenty-four-day duration of the races for up to £2,000. During this time, about 3,000 lobsters are consumed in these lodges, together with 2,000 kilograms of salmon, champagne and strawberries with cream, the snack of the genteel. The exclusive gentlemen's club White's possesses its own tent at Ascot where it serves lunch for members. Hat-designer David Shilling commented on the economic situation in 1981 as follows: 'I am working overtime. People order ever more extravagant and beautiful hats. It must be recession blues.' The waves of recession echo in the society of the rich in the form of frivolous conversational topics. Conservative MP William Rees-Davies, QC, member of numerous committees dealing with discrimination in society, hired a boat on the Thames on the occasion of the twenty-first birthday of his daughter Oonagh. The motif of the party was 'decadence'.

What is for some a motif for their celebration, is for others a reality which crushes their existence: in November 1980, eighteen-year-old Adrian Judd threw himself from a multi-storey car park, after he had been looking in vain for employment for eight months; a young woman swallowed the herbicide 'paraquat' after she had been made redundant, and the police subsequently assumed that she had committed suicide in an attack of depression; a twenty-three-year-old unemployed person burnt himself to death in Consett. The forensic scientist concluded that 'this tragic death is apparently exclusively connected with the fact that he could not find employment'. Nameless human tragedy, which has ceased to make headlines.

Great Britain is not a poor country. It has got beautifully kept landscapes and charming villages. Many towns in the Midlands and in Northern England still show some of the wounds inflicted by uncontrolled urban spread during the nineteenth century, but their character has been preserved. The slums of the industrial revolution have disappeared almost without trace. The British people command a high standard of education, and the country possesses a well-developed infrastructure. Why then is there still such misery?

Why is it that the distribution of property is so unequal that more than 90 per cent of all land is owned by only 13 per cent of the population? What is the reason for giving some directors of big companies a 'golden hand-shake' of several hundred thousand pounds on the occasion of their retirement? After all, they are able to accumulate enormous wealth from their top salaries, which are out of all proportion to the income of nearly everybody else. In 1980, a large proportion of workers earned between £60 and £100 per week. The average annual income of workers is around £6,000, some company directors receive more than £100,000 per year. Is the latter's work worth so much more? Most working people get no help with travelling expenses to and from work. Directors, however, frequently enjoy—in addition to their salaries—valuable benefits such as company cars and flats, free meals, pension contributions and private health insurance at least partially paid for by the company, subsidies towards the private education of their children etc. and additional benefits if they serve abroad. Social justice has first and foremost something to do with the just appraisal of the work of individual citizens. The upper and lower brackets of our *actual* scale of appraisal still display the gaping divergence we recognize from the period of colonialist and capitalist accumulation of wealth. It is symptomatic for society as a whole, however, if in times of crisis this huge gap is not being reduced but on the contrary deepened and increased.

CHAPTER THREE

The worker
and
industrial decline

THE BRITISH EMPIRE AND THE GENTLEMAN CAPITALIST

Britain's rise as a world power was closely connected with its former position as the world's leading trading and industrial nation. During the nineteenth century Britain was the workshop of the world. The question as to why the country, which served as the cradle of the industrial revolution, underwent such a drastic decline still dominates British public discussion. It seems peculiar, however, that with such a history the ideology and public consciousness of the country should since the nineteenth century have focused so little on its industry, technology and science. Since that date, Britain has not perceived herself primarily as a country of pioneering engineers, designers and technicians, but as the champion of civilization, democracy and freedom. In the utterances of the leading lights of the country the over-emphasis on the idea of a civilizing mission is remarkable and difficult to harmonise with questions of social and technological development.

The long career and life history of Lord Palmerston is perhaps exemplary of Britain's ruthless superpower politics during the first half of the nineteenth century. He declared in 1848 that the true policy of the country was to be 'champion of justice and right'. How was it possible to make such a claim when only a few years before Britain

violently broke China's resistance against European penetration (in the Opium War 1840–42) and had plundered
India for decades and when, at home, the democratic
demands of an impoverished working class were opposed
by the violent suppression of the Chartist movement?
Lord Palmerston was not alone in his opinion either.
Alfred Tennyson, one of the greatest English nineteenth
century writers—poet laureate of Queen Victoria—wrote
solemnly about England in his poem *You ask me why*:

> It is the land that freemen till,
>   That sober-suited Freedom chose;
>   The land, where, girt with friends or foe
> A man may speak the thing he will;
> A land of settled government,
>   A land of just and old renown,
>   Where Freedom slowly broadens down
> From precedent to precedent.

These lines invoke a free society, a society consisting of
free people who, significantly, cultivate the soil rather
than build machines. The smoking stacks and chimneys,
the railways and canals, the spinning wheels and threshing
machines are repressed from public consciousness. Instead,
the first half of the nineteenth century initiated an
astonishing revival of medieval ideals which ranged from
the knights of King Arthur's Round Table as a paragon for
modern man to the gothic style as the preferable architecture for railway stations and stock exchanges. Walter
Scott's prose elevates the knight to a hero of literature,
pre-Raphaelite paintings evoke a mythical medieval history
as the true epoch of human greatness, and even an artist
as politically aware as William Morris resisted the barbarity
of his age by drawing upon elements of artistic style and
manufacturing methods dating back to the pre-industrial
era. If one studied the nineteenth century with the help
of these phenomena alone, one would hardly guess that
Britain had anything at all to do with the industrial revolu-

tion or indeed with colonial exploitation. It is quite astonishing that a nation's perception of itself can be so unclear about its real situation and material basis—without this perception being felt as a contradiction, not to mention self-deception.

The repression of industry, technology and science from public perception had two decisive social consequences. Firstly, poverty, injustice and the condition of the working class generally were also ousted from public consciousness. Secondly, and quite paradoxically, Britain did not develop a national, leading industrial class. The low social esteem enjoyed by industry and technology led to the fact that the British elite regarded industrial activities as unworthy. Hence, they aimed at leading positions within the British Empire or at the speedy acquisition of a landed estate. Martin J. Wiener in his work *English Culture and the Decline of the Industrial Spirit* (1981) argues that Britain's gradual economic decline can be traced back, among other factors, to the fact that since 1850 businessmen and industrialists enjoyed less and less public esteem and that it therefore became unattractive to make a career in manufacturing. A kind of 'gentleman-industrialist' therefore developed, who quite consciously adopted the attitude of an amateur and who ran his own factory as a hobby. The desirable, primary preoccupation remained simply to be 'gentleman'. The manufacturing sector of the economy was nearly taboo. The alliance between the aristocracy and the bourgeoisie during the nineteenth century led to a comprehensive penetration of aristocratic ideals into middle class thinking. The unique institution of the public schools succeeded in achieving the 'aristocratization' of the bourgeoisie within a very short space of time, affecting both their thinking and their activities. During the second half of the nineteenth century, the British bourgeoisie aimed to ape the aristocratic landowner and hence invested in land rather than factories. For Martin J. Wiener, the British aristocracy had won a clandestine cultural victory over the increasingly dominating bourgeoisie: 'As capitalists became landed gentlemen, JPs, and men of breeding, the radical ideal of active capital was submerged in the conservative ideal of passive property, and the urge to enterprise faded beneath the preference for stability.' (Wiener, 1981, p. 14.)

The infection of the middle classes with aristocratic ideals encroached also upon the professions—law, medicine and higher education as well as the civil service, journalism and literature. Most leading representatives of the intelligentsia had attended public schools, and they enjoyed a kind of upbringing there which had little to do with conventional ideas about school education. The great reformer of public schools, Dr Thomas Arnold, headmaster of Rugby Public School, introduced at the beginning of the nineteenth century the concept of education as the 'shaping of character'. Dr Arnold still understood his approach against the background of a general humanist education, but during the decades to come the ideal of 'shaping the character' became an end in itself and was reduced to the 'shaping of leadership qualities'. Knowledge and intelligence took second place, the emphasis was on proper conduct and the ability to command others. Physical education assumed a dominant position, and to this day many public school pupils excel rather more as captains of rugby and cricket teams and rather less in mathematics, physics or modern languages. Also, sporting activities such as these served primarily the purpose of 'shaping the character' as opposed to the acquisition of physical strength. To this day cricket is regarded as the archetype for a gentleman's sport. 'Ideal' traits of character were circulated in numerous books and pamphlets. Novels like *Tom Brown's Schooldays* by Thomas Hughes, published in 1857, belonged to the favourite literature of generations of students attending both public and grammar schools (the latter were trying to emulate public school ideals). It is the story of a student at Rugby under Dr Thomas Arnold's headmastership. Tom Brown is the son of a lord of the manor. It does not matter to his father if his son does not acquire 'decent Greek' while at school. The main thing is that his son will grow up to become a 'decent, helpful Englishman who always tells the truth, a gentleman as well as a Christian'. The story is an ideological model for public school upbringing. In this book, public school leavers become priests or enter the legal profession or assume responsibilities 'under the Indian sun or in Australian towns and glades'. Trade or industry are not mentioned. A professional existence in these areas is not regarded as being in keeping with their social standing.

It is dangerous for any ruling class when knowledge and intelligence are looked on with disdain and are abandoned to the ambitious. The English expression 'he is a character' contains even today the connotation that a person deserves appreciation on the basis of his personality (or character), even if he lacks professional skills. In the past the administration of the Empire required completely different qualities and 'personality or character' meant in this context the capacity to cope with Indian rebellion or with a Sudanese uprising. Numerous incidents were re-written in the spirit of colonialist ideology for school students and cadets to emulate. Often the story is of a courageous English officer who bravely faces armed rebels in the colonies unarmed and who squashes any resistance merely by the force of his personal authority.

There are innumerable stories of noble knights, modelled on the allegory of Saint George, the patron saint of England. Saint George, who vanquished the dragon, became the archetypal symbol of a Christian hero who wins victory over evil. The noble knight as paragon and hero reappears during the consolidation of the Empire in many variations: in wall paintings, book illustrations, stained glass windows and monuments. Some members of the aristocracy even had castles, armours and weapons built for them which were all faithful imitations of medieval models. It was as if King Arthur and the knights of his Round Table had re-awakened. This sort of medieval revivalism made any intellectual engagement with the realities of the time very difficult, realities shaped by the industrial revolution and the beginnings of the labour movement. Lieutenant-General Robert Baden-Powell, educated at Charterhouse Public School, officer in India and Africa, became famous as founder of the boy scout movement. He called the boy scouts 'the young knights of the Empire'. Just as medieval knights crusaded against the 'pagans' from the east to defend Christian culture, so the British people fight as modern knights on the outer posts of the Empire in order to spread civilization and defeat barbarism. In a collection of speech day addresses by an English headmaster during the 1930s, entitled *Give me a Character, Sir*, modern colonial knights are incorporated in the tradition of medieval knights. Examples for the young school-leavers include: Roland, who fought against the Saracens; the Black Prince in the battle against the French; Sir Philip Sidney in the war against the Spanish and General Charles Gordon in his military expedition against the Arabs of East Africa. One address by the head-master closes with the words: 'May we all grow up to become modern knights. . . Amen.' In an intellectual atmosphere dominated by the combined myths of gentle-men and knights, it is hardly surprising that the British ruling class becomes a victim of its own legends. Martin Wiener calls the development of these aristocratic-bourgeois ideals of civilization, which continue to live on, 'the cultural counter-revolution'.

The British gentleman-capitalist cannot cope with the challenge his own capitalist environment poses. By his very attitude, he negates the very law under which he set out to conduct his day-to-day affairs. His right-wing criticism of capitalism hinders the development of the means of production. The chairman of Rolls Royce indignantly responded in 1969 to the question whether it was the purpose of his company to make profit: 'If you said we're here to make profits, we'd never be making aeroengines: we'd have gone into property years ago.' (Wiener, 1981, p. 141.) Only two years later Rolls Royce was bankrupt.

Two major attitudes shape the gentleman-capitalist. Either the ethos of 'pure engineering' is maintained, as in the case of Rolls Royce, as if the question of marketing was vulgar, or the field of manufacturing itself is looked down upon and only the higher world of finance is regarded as an acceptable field of a activity. In both cases, the attitude may be described as a schizophrenic one, wherein money is earned in a kind of immaculate conception. There is furthermore either no room for the production process and for the workers themselves or both are dealt with as unpleasant secondary phenomena.

To this day British capitalism has been only partially successful in training an elite who actually feels a contradiction between the requirements of technical and industrial change and their own cultural and social values. A 1981 study on British management entitled *British Corporate Leaders* concludes that still more than 60 per cent of the leading directors in British industry have taken their university degrees in arts subjects unconnected with their work. According to this study, only 3 per cent of higher British management see good prospects for profits and promotion in the manufacturing sector of the economy. On the other hand, more than 50 per cent regard the world of trade and finance as the 'fastest route to the top'. In this way, not only many talented capitalists are lost to the manufacturing sector of the economy, but also the capital necessary for its renewal. Capital tends to flow into the City rather than into the construction of new factories.

INDUSTRIAL REFORM OF THE NEW RIGHT

In 1959, the highly regarded novelist C.P. Snow complained about the lethargic and helpless approach of the British ruling class in a comparison he made with the decline of the Republic of Venice:

I can't help thinking of the Venetian Republic in their last half-century. Like us, they had once been fabulously lucky. They had become rich, as we did, by accident. They had acquired immense political skill, just as we have. A good many of them were tough-minded, realistic, patriotic men. They knew, just as clearly as we know, that the current of history had begun to flow against them. Many of them gave their minds to working out ways to keep going. It would have meant breaking the pattern into which they had crystallised. They were fond of the pattern, just as we are fond of ours. They never found the will to break it. (Wiener, 1981, p. 141.)

This 'mood of eclipse' in ruling circles is still characteristic of the general attitude to the fate of the nation. The 1979 Conservative manifesto contends right at the beginning that Great Britain was 'a great country which seems to have lost its way'. The New Right under Mrs Margaret Thatcher proposed a programme for the 'breaking up of old structures' as radical as that of the British Left. Mrs Thatcher begins with the supposition that 'the nation is living beyond its means', and that more money is spent than is earned by production. The only new thing in her position is that she does not just mean the employees, but the employers as well. The technocratically oriented New Right has chosen the United States of America and the Federal Republic of Germany as its models. According to Mrs Thatcher, Great Britain suffers from a 'why work syndrome'. Her efforts are radical not only in their attempts to curtail trade union rights and to break the unions' power within the companies—this has been equally pursued by Mrs Thatcher's Conservative predecessors—but also in her policy of letting uncompetitive companies go bankrupt. Her Conservative government has therefore deliberately raised the threshold of competitiveness: firstly, via cuts in investment subsidies and secondly, via a virtually unprecedented rise in interest rates. The lame ducks were thus purposely deprived of their crutches in order to force them either to learn running again or to give up 'the race' altogether. Mrs Thatcher wants to have her measures understood in terms of a return to 'old-fashioned principles', like 'sound money and good house-keeping'. The New Right has broken with social democratic ideas of state management of the economy, which characterized the consensus politics of the past. The New Right favours instead, and has begun to implement, a very comprehensive privatization programme of public assets and public companies, ranging from local government institutions and services to the profitable parts of steel production and aircraft construction. The policies of the New Right are also remarkable for being directed against unprogressive employers. They say that the bacillus 'socialism' has also infected British management who give in to union pressure and agree to working practices which made the regaining of competitiveness impossible. Too many workers were working too little or too restrictedly. On 23 February 1982, Mrs Thatcher declared in a speech at the Engineering Employers Federation dinner at the Dorchester Hotel, London: 'If two people do the work of one, both stand to lose their jobs. Restrictive practices and overmanning once designed to save jobs have lost whole factories. And even whole industries. This kind of unemployment cannot possibly be ascribed to governments. It is due to attitudes in industry.'

The New Right has achieved some success with the argument that former working practices had to be abandoned, not least because the methods of previous prime ministers to halt economic decline had been largely unsuccessful. The successful implementation of Mrs Thatcher's ruthless austerity measures may also be explained from the fact that social democratic promises of a just and prosperous market economy under the general aegis of the state have so far not been fulfilled.

Unemployment figures of several million are the most tangible and the most serious consequence of Conservative policies to restructure the economy. At the level of companies, unemployment destroys the slowly developed structures of organized labour. The strength of organized groups in companies largely depends on personal relationships and on trust in leadership, both of which have to develop over the years, especially during disputes. In many companies, unemployment has led to a serious erosion of such informal structures of organized labour. One specific example of this is the deliberate destruction of the influence exercised by some shop stewards in British Leyland. The case of the communist shop steward Derek Robinson, 'Red Robbo', who was dismissed in 1979, underlines the means at the disposal of employers, despite legislation designed to protect workers, once the workers' inclination to fight was weakened by rising unemployment. Derek Robinson had been dismissed because he, among others, had signed an alternative austerity plan for British Leyland. Despite massive protest and all efforts by his union he was not reinstated. Since that time, militancy in the car-making industry has decreased noticeably.

Mrs Thatcher's Conservative Government expressively set out to undo the special position of the unions in public law. The Conservatives have carefully and over a long period drafted legislation designed to lift immunity during industrial disputes which has been legally guaranteed since 1906. The intention is to make industrial disputes more and more amenable to court settlement so that ideally lawyers on both sides negotiate pay claims, benefits and improvement of working conditions in front of judges.

This has the effect of transforming unions from fighting organizations at the level of companies to pressure groups in the corridors of companies and ministries.

Since their beginnings during the nineteenth century, the unions have been 'schools of consciousness' for workers, who by practical actions became more familiar with the wider social aims and purposes of the labour movement. For most workers, industrial disputes are practically the only real possibility to play an active political role. Collective bargaining at the level of companies, strikes and other forms of disputes are the major means of emancipation and self-reliance of workers, both individually and as a class. It is towards this vital nerve of organized labour that the measures of the New Right are directed.

PRAXIS OF INDUSTRIAL WORKERS

One of the basic problems facing all workers in their resistance to these policies is the unequal development of industrial sectors. In some branches of industry the most modern equipment and working methods as well as the closed shop operate, whereas in others the most archaic conditions still predominate. The consequences are often rivalries and injustices among parts of the working class. In most great British ports, the system of working for daily wages was largely abolished only during the 1960s. Only since 1968 are there official shop stewards and national negotiating committees for dock workers. Some ports (such as Hull) are still so-called non-registered ports, however, and have maintained the system of day labourers. The results of this unequal development are undercut wages, the use of strike breakers and much unnecessary bad blood among workers, who are constantly forced into competition with one another. Dock worker and trade unionist Jack Dash describes in his autobiography *Good Morning, Brothers* the daily fight, every morning, of individual gangs, for an order. Jack Dash illustrates such a scene in London docks from the perspective of somebody seeking employment:

Across the road the foremen are synchronising their watches. Some of the men are practising hypnotism, staring at the back of the neck of a particular foreman in the hope that when he turns round they'll be the first one he'll catch sight of and call on. At another place of call, you'll perhaps hear the fly-boys remarking that such-and-such a firm has got a good job—hoping that some of the inexperienced youngsters will rush down to that place of call and leave this one clear for the fly-boys.

All of a sudden there is a complete hush. Everyone is standing still, expectant and anxious. The smaller men at the rear stand on tiptoe. Over walk the ship and quay foremen, like a Sheriff's posse in a Western. Charlie's gang! Smith's gang! Four men for *pro rate* on chilled beef! There is a rush and a flurry, arms are outstretched with registration books in the hands (without the registration book you can't go to work). The little men in the front have been shoved aside. When there's been a heavy spell of unemployment, the call-on reminds you of a flock of seagulls converging on a morsel.

(Dash 1970, p. 100.)

Every day the fight for work, every day the renewed worry whether one will earn sufficient money, and every day some workers go home without finding work.

The example of the gangs shows how fatally two things can come together: an obsolete organizational principle within the company on the one hand, and on the other an achievement: that workers may at least partially organize their own work themselves. The same situation has both positive and negative aspects, which have to be distinguished when it comes to assessing industrial disputes. Working in gangs or small groups is quite common in many branches of industry and has in principle nothing to do with day labouring, short-time work or obsolete working practises. Gangs or crews are a natural form of organization. They represent the human or social counterpart to the complex technological side of the working process. However, this principle may have very negative effects on the entire climate of work as well as on the individual demand for work, if employers play off workers against each other. Journalist Martin Leighton writes about the fixed code of practice, which has crystallized among gang workers as an unwritten law, in his documentary report *Men at Work* which is about the lives of British labourers:

If you needed advice, you asked a mate; if there was a decision to make, you discussed it with a mate; if good work were ever recognised and praised, it would be by a mate. Our rules of behaviour were imposed from within, a tacitly understood code of manners and courtesies which have close parallels with the rules of the class-room: you cover for your mates, and never on any account say any-thing which might get them into trouble/*do not sneak*; never work competitively in order to show up your mates/*do not be a swot*; on the other hand, do a sufficient share of work so nobody gets into trouble/*do not be a slacker*; take care never to try to appear superior to others/*do not swank*.   (Leighton, 1981, p. 57.)

Martin Leighton reports on construction workers in this case, but similar relationships emerge wherever people have to cooperate to construct a ship, to build a road, to mine coal or to cast metal. Automation and mechanization, however, radically altered working methods. Containers in ports and mechanical extraction equipment in the mining industry have drastically changed the physical working conditions of workers since the end of World War II. In recent years, industrial disputes have frequently been not about pay, but about the introduction of new technologies and working practices. Disputes in the printing and railway industries are good examples of this. The emphasis here lies particularly on the conditions rather than technology itself. Resistance against technological change is often branded as a form of modern Luddism by the media. Today's workers are seen as acting like the Luddites who smashed mechanical weaving looms in the North of England around 1815 because these were taking away their daily bread and employment. The protest then was not, of course, directed blindly against the machines themselves, but against the loss of the basis of their existence. Today, similarly, resistance against the introduction of automated processes is a result of the fact that the redistribution of employment is not regulated for society as a whole. In our society the contradiction persists that improved work processes through technological progress usually leave some individuals destitute and some overworked. Even if all the staff is kept, the introduction of new machinery always brings with it the problem of reorganization of the human side of the working process. Time limits for the execution of manufacturing processes are laid down, usually as a result of long negotiations. If workers sometimes seem to stick stubbornly to obsolete practices, then this is to be explained from their experience that modernization has so often been used as a lever to extract yet further advantage from their capacity to work. When, for example, a data processor equipped with screen and printer changes the journalist into both a printer and a typesetter, or when operators of drilling machines are given control over the whole assembly line, then what is in principle a facilitation of work can lead to added difficulties for the individual. This question may not always be foreseen when new machinery is introduced, and the more complicated and up-to-date the equipment the more care has to be taken to regulate the human side of the work process. This problem has always existed when new technologies are introduced and has in itself nothing to do with computers and microprocessors as such. The mechanical weaving looms were followed by automatic spinning machines. These all represented facilitations of work generally, but they also brought increased exploitation of individuals.

The complex nature of technological change and the huge, concomitant human problems are not adequately reported by journalistic accounts of the world of work. British newspapers are full of industrial stories, but industrial disputes are primarily represented as rows over pay or productivity which have nothing to do with the great questions concerning the economic renewal of the country. The weekly magazine *The Economist*, a con-servative, pro-American and technologically orientated publication, succinctly expressed this attitude in a report on the 1980 steel strike: 'The dispute on pay or pro-ductivity looks daily more and more like a dispute over the deckchairs on the *Titanic*.' Many strikes are– in truth– industrial disputes over basic questions of economic orientation. The three-month-long steel strike of 1980 was primarily about the gradual dismantlement and privatization of the British steel industry. Everything was done from the official side to make it seem that this dispute was the result of union actions and merely reflected their eagerness to strike. One of the highest judges in Great Britain, Lord Denning, who in the name of *'common-sense'* made hardly credible, politically motivated judgements, passed an injunction against the steel workers' union and forbade the strike. His reasoning read: 'The disastrous consequences of such a strike for the economy and the well-being of the country mean that the court is right in passing this injunction in order to prevent these people laying down their work and picketing.' Lord Denning's decision in this case was later overruled after appeal to the House of Lords, but the wording of Lord Denning's judgement clearly demonstrates that the right to strike will be undermined by dealing with industrial disputes as legal cases.

Although most people are employed and thereby have some experience of the world of work, the latter is still unknown territory as far as public consciousness is concerned. In addition there are many companies surrounded by secrets. Some plants, like the big car-makers Ford, British Leyland and General Motors refuse point blank to admit journalists. The reason is that relations between management and workers are too tense for them to be displayed publicly. If one sets out to look for the voice of workers in the daily reports of the media, one finds only arbitrarily chosen, fragmentary utterances, which make little sense in the illusory world of the media. Journalists like Martin Leighton and Jeremy Seabrook have nevertheless composed documentaries on the lives of workers, both at home and in their factories. These reports do document a high level of consciousness among workers, despite the phenomena of resignation, lack of interest and persistence of class differences. Jeremy Seabrook's book *What Went Wrong?* contains numerous life stories, told by male and female workers from all parts of the country. Mrs Grace Ryan, in her mid forties, talks about the consequences of piece-work in a plastics factory in London. She has been employed in this company for twenty-six years:

Piece-work makes workers selfish. A lot of them would work right through the dinner hour and the tea-breaks. You have to see that doesn't happen, because it would make a difference to the piece-work grades. They don't like it. Or perhaps if the machine guard falls off and has to be fitted, they'd rather work without the guard, you have to stop them. That's the incentive you see, to risk your safety, to jeopardize other people's work levels. It encourages you to compete with the machine. If you're not careful you find yourself becoming like the machine. You imitate it, cold unfeeling lumps of metal. The tea-breaks are precious anyway. They're really our chance for a bit of comradeship. . . You know what it is—the machine makes you passive and lethargic in your mind. You suspend your life while you're at work, and then an awful lot of your leisure is like a repeat performance of work, part of the same process. I'm sometimes afraid that the leisure revolution is going to be a tranquillized half-life. Already a lot of people are never really awake; not awake to the real possibilities the way life could be.

(Seabrook, 1978, pp. 216–17.)

There is a consistent, highly conscious feeling among workers that they come low down the social scale of society and its values, that they are being pushed out, told what to do, at the receiving end of commands from others.

Disease, malnutrition and over-working caused the physical disintegration of working class people during the nineteenth century. H. G. Wells invokes in his famous novel *The Time Machine* a clear vision of the physical as well as the psychological consequences of class divisions. His hero, a traveller in time, finds in the future only the ruins of civilization, like the ghost-like ruins of the great London museums. People have degenerated into two different races, which have become enemies: the working creatures live underground and fear the light, and elfin-like creatures live overground, they are weak and incapable of looking after themselves.

Since the nineteenth century the working class has fought hard for its rights and secured many tangible achievements, driving back poverty and despair. However, given the enormous possibilities of today's society these achievements still seem rather small, and should certainly not be used to disguise some of the crude forms of exploitation which still persist. Especially for some of the older workers exploitation remains part of their life history. Many achievements of the workers' movement which we take for granted today are not even one generation old, and today seem under renewed threat.

WORKING MEN'S CULTURE:
THE *BALLAD OF JOHN AXON*

The development of working men's culture plays an important role in the struggle for the progressive emancipation of the working class. The Federation of Worker Writers and Community Publishers, which publishes the magazine *Voices*, has an important coordinating function for the various groups of worker artists in contemporary England. The artistic assimilation of the life experiences of 'the lower classes' has undergone considerable development since World War II. Unknown, non-professional writers, such as J. Clifford in his poem *Photographs* display a high level of artistic expression:

> I have seen you before somewhere;
> Were you not third from the left
> In that faded photograph,
> Among the others in khaki
> Or stiff in suits and cloth caps?
> And did you not die on the barbed wire,
> Or deep in the mine, or deep in the workhouse.
> Or in some long forgotten rebellion,
> Brave when others were brave?
> I cannot remember.
> Yet I have seen you before
> Many, many times;
> In the pub, on the picket line,
> The dole queue, the supermarket,
> The works outing.
> And not just here either.

Did you not march out one winter morning
And dig trenches to defend Moscow?
And did you not ride the boxcars
Into Oregon through the rain?
And did you not picnic one spring day
In your sunday trousers on the banks of the Seine?
Friend, your name is lost for ever, and yet
Any mirror will tell me
Where I have seen you before!

(*Voices* 23, 1981, p. 8.)

The anonymity of simple people is in stark contrast to the so-called personalities created almost daily by the media. Quizzes on radio and television ask about the most obscure names in show business, pop music or politics. Simple people and their lives have no place in this kind of publicity.

Every ten years a great man.	Alle zehn Jahre ein grosser Mann.
Who pays the expenses?	Wer bezahlt die Spesen?
So many reports,	So viele Berichte,
So many questions,	So viele Fragen,

says Bertolt Brecht in his poem *Fragen eines lesenden Arbeiters* (questions of a reading worker). A satirical revival of these lines by Max von der Grün concludes tersely: 'In eight years of schooling we did not learn how to ask.'

The voices of workers have been captured uniquely and successfully in Ewan MacColl's and Charles Parker's radio ballads. Ewan MacColl is one of the most important song writers and interpreters of the English folk movement since World War II. Charles Parker was a radio director with the BBC. They completed eight radio ballads between 1957 and 1964. These ballads really represent one of the most original artistic assimilations of the life and working experiences of simple people: railwaymen, miners, fishermen, street builders, polio victims, boxers, youngsters, gypsies.

After World War II, Ewan MacColl and Joan Littlewood, who was then his wife, founded the theatre group *Theatre Workshop*. He wrote plays like *Johnny Noble*, the history of a seaman set against the background of the Depression of the 1930s, the Spanish Civil War and World War II itself. These plays were committed to the English music hall tradition on the one hand and to the German and Russian traditions of political agitation on the other. Until 1953 the *Theatre Workshop* travelled up and down the country and performed their plays in pubs, churches and clubrooms. Later, they moved into a Victorian theatre in Stratford, East London, and developed into one of the leading avant-garde companies of the country. Ewan MacColl, however, felt this step of settling down to be the first step towards integration into the established theatre world and hence abandonment of the ideal of a truly proletarian theatre close to the people. He separated from his wife, left the theatre and devoted himself to the collection and interpretation of worker songs. His LP record *The Steel Whistle Ballads*, which was released then, is a classic of the folk movement. Together with his new partner Peggy Seeger, sister of the American folk singer Pete Seeger, he sought to extend the effectiveness of the song as a publicly appealing means of expression.

In the United States, Norman Corwin and Earl Robinson had meanwhile composed so-called folk cantata for radio. *Ballad for Americans* and *The Lonesome Train* are examples of this. Pete Seeger had also modified workers' songs and their themes for broadcasting purposes. This kind of ballad now became known in Britain, partly through Charles Parker's work for the North American service of the BBC. Charles Parker and Ewan MacColl received an assignment from the BBC (in the autumn of 1957) to write a documentary on train driver John Axon, who had been fatally wounded in February of the same year. At this point, neither Parker nor MacColl had any idea about the new kind of radio ballad which were to eventually emerge from their work.

On 9 February 1957, two freight trains had collided near Manchester. In the train driven by John Axon the brakes failed completely due to a big crack in the steam pipe. As there was a natural downward slope, the train and its 33 loaded cargo carriages were rolling towards a track section used by a passenger train. John Axon remained in the driver's cabin in order to warn a signalman of the threatening accident and in the hope of regaining control of his train once it had passed the slope. All travellers in the passenger train were successfully taken to safety, but it was too late to warn a second, waiting freight train. The collision cost the lives of both John Axon and another railwayman in the second freight train.

Initially, Ewan MacColl and Charles Parker attempted to dramatize John Axon's life history in a way analogous to the literary ballad. The American folk tradition with its glorification of the folk hero as a legendary figure also served as an example. However, within a short space of time, the planned documentary on train driver John Axon developed into something completely different: a ballad on both the work and the people involved with the railways. The taped material which they recorded in engine sheds and on the trains themselves, was of such originality as well as lyric quality that old forms of ballads were given up easily. Workers told about their attitudes and sensations connected with engines as well as the countryside they drove in with such amazing expressiveness that responsible BBC editors hardly believed their authenticity. It was even presumed at some point that MacColl and Parker had been putting words into the mouths of railwaymen. It was ignorantly argued that only professional writers were capable of verbally expressing such subtle experiences. In one of the most famous sequences of the *Ballad of John Axon*, train driver Jack Pickford describes his sensations when taking his steam engine out into open country at dawn. Jack Pickford had initially told his story in a pub against a somewhat noisy background. When he was asked the next morning whether he could perhaps repeat the whole thing, he readily retold what he had to say in several variations which became better and better.

When it comes to recording workers, there is the general attitude among broadcasters that you would have to apply the method of the 'wild-life hide' in order to get original comments. However, clandestine listening—applicable to observation of wild animals—was not the way here. Jack Pickford's sequence indicates a highly conscious assimilation of how he relates to the world in which he lives and works. This sequence at dawn is given below, it was rendered in a Midlands accent, with effective pauses and lengthening of the vowels, with dramatic humour in his voice as well as quiet solemnity:

What a feeling you have when you get off the shed; you've got the engine, you've got the control of it, and what a feeling—I'm cock of the bank, there's nobody who can take a rise out of me now, she's mine. Come on me old beauty and off we go. The moon's out and the countryside—it's lovely. Look at that hill over there with the moon shining on it and the trees and the valley. It's beautiful. On we go, what a feeling—she answers to every touch. Some more rock on, lad. Yes—it's grand. Oh look they're lit up in the mill across the way, somebody else is working on nights besides us. Look there, the sun's coming over the hills. And what a sight. England at dawn. It's been worth losing a night's sleep for, this has. If only the people of England could see it. England. . . England. And there's nowhere like it at dawn.   (MacColl, 1958.)

Jack Pickford is clearly very proud to work with such a strong and powerful engine, which responds to every touch, and this pride as well as the happiness about his independence as a free man in free nature are both perceived in a more-than-personal way as a sense of belonging to the national community: the love of the engine, nature, his country and his people flow together to form a unity.

Original recordings such as these made MacColl and Parker eschew traditional documentary techniques. They had originally intended to use verbal sequences only as research material or for background effects. At best, they thought initially, some selected quotable passages could be read out by actors. However, the stories of these workers and their original voices proved to be so expressive that they were elevated to shape the central element of the dramatized radio ballad. The second and still more important innovation was the elimination of a neutral narrator who would lead the listener from event to event. In fact, every kind of comment—explanatory, transitional or otherwise—was deliberately omitted. Such a documentary required a new dramaturgy as it consisted purely of original recordings. The new linking element between individual sequences were to be song and music. Instead of using music conventionally as a mere introduction to, or illustration of, a particular passage, music was allocated a narrative function in these radio ballads. It was closely interwoven with the original recordings of workers, sometimes without transition.

Radio ballads are not documentaries but artistic radio plays, which use the authentic utterances of workers and puts these quotations together, by means of comprehensive montage, to form a new and unique whole. The four main composite elements (original recordings, song, sound effects, instrumental music) are combined to produce an hour-long feature. Although the radio ballad was developed only about twenty years ago, it has already been responsible for several productions of clear historic and documentary value, particularly for sectors of industrial life which have either undergone considerable change (like the coal mining industry), or which have virtually died out (like the herring fishing industry).

THE BIG HEWER ON THE GROUND OF THE OCEAN

The Big Hewer is a radio ballad on the miners. With this ballad, Ewan MacColl and Charles Parker have created a kind of industrial saga, a piece of history of the British labour movement. The development of coal mining is exemplary for studying industrialization generally. Miners represent one of the most militant and one of the most conscious parts of the British working class. The constitution of *the National Union of Mineworkers (NUM)* talks explicitly about the clear objective to achieve, together with other organizations: the complete abolition of capitalism.

To promote and secure the passing of legislation for improving the condition of the members and ensuring them a guaranteed week's wage with protective clauses for the miners even when they cease work, when cessation is due to causes beyond the immediate control of the members, and to join in with other organisations for the purpose of and with the view to the complete abolition of Capitalism.

(Rules, Model Rules, Standing Orders.
National Union of Mineworkers; 1978.)

The history of miners is also the history of child labour, the Tommy shops, the Chartist movement and, particularly, of hard, dangerous, intensely physical labour, which was quite paradoxically a result of the industrial revolution. The forging of chains, for example, required the manual use of hammers weighing several metric hundredweights. The work in front of limekilns corroded the lungs and eyes of the young workers, who did not live much beyond twenty years. There have been times when the entire coal industry employed more than 1.5 million people; today it is only about 250,000 people and declining. D.H. Lawrence's famous novel *Sons and Lovers* describes the mining milieu as a paradigm for the life conditions and aspirations of the working class during the closing stages of the nineteenth century. Then, everybody came in touch with coal in some way or another: from the worker, who extracted it, to the gentleman, who made use of it in his fireplace. Coal physically blackened whole cities and countrysides and was extractable in some parts of Britain just underneath the surface of the ground, so most people had direct experience of it. In the Black Country, the industrial area between Birmingham and Wolverhampton, coal often occurred in mining seams ten meters thick; it was therefore frequently extracted by digging holes. These were gradually dug deeper, one next to the other, similar to ordinary wells. The area was so rich in coal that it was hardly worth constructing underground shafts.

After the end of World War II many workers' houses were knocked down as part of urban redevelopment programmes. In the Black Country many houses needed only a few knocks by bulldozers in order to be virtually rased to the ground. The entire rubble disappeared underground. It emerged thereafter that many families had constructed a 'mini pit' in their cellars, i.e. the cellar 'floor' consisted of pure coal. Supplies were extracted from the ground with shovel and pickaxe. Even today, streets in the Black Country subside all of a sudden, because long forgotten shafts and drifts had been built over without adequate support.

A.L. Lloyd, singer, collector and historian of folk songs, has rescued many miners' songs from oblivion and recorded them under the title *Come all ye bold miners*. He also participated in the production of *The Big Hewer*, as did other well-known folk-song interpreters such as Ian Campbell and Louis Killen. As with other radio ballads, *The Big Hewer* came into being by cooperation between workers and professional artists. The introduction to the ballad said that the audience was about to listen to a 'legend, told by miners from South Wales, from the Midlands, from Northumberland and from Durham'. This 'legend' is the story told by Temble, the big hewer, a giant miner, who performed super-human achievements in his work. His pickaxe is heard all the time, without interruption. Temble is a legendary figure who never actually existed. He represents the archetypal miner who serves as a mirror for the professional ethos of every individual miner. This legend is only a framework mentioned right at the beginning and at the end of *The Big Hewer*, the actual radio ballad itself deals with the story of a typical miner's working life: descending for the first time into a shaft; the first experiences underground; the perpetual fear of an accident; the physical demands; the gradual enfeeblement through silicosis and, again and again, the human relationship with coal and its extraction. The miners find very expressive metaphors for their lives underground. One miner describes the stillness down a shaft like being 'on the floor of the ocean'. Another said that he was not only a miner through and through, but he had lived so closely with and around coal that black blood would flow if he cut his finger. And a third miner remarked about coal itself:

Coal is a thing that costs life to get. You may be holding a piece of coal in your hand and turn it around and say, I wonder how that coal was got. Was there any blood shedding on that coal? Was there any man's life lost in it? And there is many a one in this country who has put coal on the fire there has been a man's life lost on it. You are not burning coal, you are burning blood.   (MacColl, 1962.)

The technique of the radio ballad sets free the poetic quality of these sentences by taking them out of the context of the original recording and putting them into the new context of the radio ballad as independent quotations. Although the tunes of the songs used are derived from traditional folk music, their texts have been rewritten by MacColl. In doing so, he incorporated what miners said and thereby linked the individual sequences.

This linking technique is original because the audience gains the impression that the worker is speaking out at the coal-face without the disturbing and distancing presence of an interviewer. In principle the radio ballad relies on journalistic reportage, but it is significantly different from reportage in the artistic modification of the original recordings. MacColl and Parker used the utterances of miners sparingly. Most sequences do not take longer than fifteen to twenty seconds each. A whole life story may at times be condensed to a single sentence, but this succinct treatment may reveal more of the life-drama of the speaker than long-winded descriptions. For example, there is the conversation of several miners about their first time down the shaft which finds the seemingly abrupt addition: 'I hated it, I hated it from the very first day on.' It is the voice of one of the older miners with the largest share of his active life behind him. Although the voice sounded firm and strong, it was clearly the voice of someone who never forgot that he was not allowed to choose his profession, and that he therefore had to live a life which he could not really accept as his own.

LABOUR DISPUTES OF THE 1970s

It was only during the past few decades that the everyday life of workers has been researched systematically. In this context, local libraries have become absolutely essential archives for regional historical research in Britain. Even small libraries in the industrial villages of the Black Country or of the South Welsh mining villages frequently possess irreplaceable documents of the history of workers: photographic collections of families, post-cards, personal letters as well as invoice and order books of companies which have closed down long ago. The documents were often kept by pure chance. Since many local libraries themselves have a history of more than one hundred years, they often contain rare monographs from the nineteenth century. Some of these libraries were founded by philantropic millionaires, such as the American steel king Andrew Carnegie who, as a born Scotsman, dedicated part of his wealth for charity purposes to Great Britain. These documents have still not been systematically collected and researched, although photographs are now published more frequently.

A good example of this is John Gorman's volume *To Build Jerusalem* (1980). The author is a printer by profession, and he presented selected photographs from 1875 to 1950 accompanied by information on the relevant historical background. One of the last photographs in this collection show an old miner with his lamp, wearing tattered work-clothes standing beside the banner of the newly founded, publicly owned National Coal Board (NCB) in 1947. This is John Gorman's comment on the picture:

The photograph of George Short, who was born in 1872 and started work underground at the age of twelve, perfectly enshrines the mood of 1947. In his face, a life of work and hardship, proudly alongisde the banner of the NCB, the mines for the people, hope realised at the end of a working life, a dignified conclusion and a better beginning.   (Gorman, 1980, p. 185.)

It was only during World War II that about forty individual mining unions had agreed on the foundation of a single union embracing the entire coal industry. The subsequent nationalization of the industry brought the beginnings of some form of union participation in the running of one of the country's key industries. Nationalization of the coal industry terminated the semi-feudal conditions in many pits where aristocratic mine owners ruled like kings over the coal miners. The history of owner domination fits badly with the picture of a centuries-old democracy and civilization in Great Britain found in apologetic histories. The 'coal lords' included: Lord Rhondda and Lord Merthyr of Senghenydd in South Wales; Lord Lambton in Durham; Lord Aberconway and the Markham family in Derbyshire; the Duke of Hamilton and Count Dalkeith in Scotland; Major Barber in Nottinghamshire. Trained miner Lewis Jones provided a classic literary portrait of such a coal owner in the two parts of the novel *Cwmardy*, who ruled like an absolute prince over life and death in mining villages.

Today, the *National Union of Mineworkers* (NUM) is a strongly politicized union, whose industrial struggles and positions on questions of the national economy often signal the way for the trade union movement as a whole. The first two decades after nationalization of the coal industry were dominated by the struggle against comprehensive pit closure programmes. From 1945 until 1970, the number of miners fell from 500,000 to about 290,000. At the same time, wages in the industry declined below the standard of the rest of the economy. The structure of this nationalized industry was new and its position within the production sector of the economy was unique for a long time. Hence it took the experience of ten to twenty years to realize that nationalization by itself had neither changed the capitalist character of the coal industry nor did it automatically protect miners from a deterioration of their standard of living or of their working conditions. There was an increasing number of people within the NUM who demanded the abandonment of loyalty to the present leadership. The trade union movement generally shifted to the left during the 1970s after the somewhat disillusioning 1964–1970 Labour governments. More radical figures within the NUM gained influence and criticized the NUM leadership for collaboration.

These and other protests at grassroot level were to lead to an important shift of power within the whole British trade union movement. The NUM was perhaps the most radical protagonist in this process. The arguments between the right and left wings of this union began at the beginning of the 1970s and happened against the background of some of the most far-reaching industrial disputes in post-war history. Between 1971 and 1974, the left-wing unions succeeded in persuading their colleagues to give up passive resistance to Prime Minister Edward Heath's Conservative Government and enter active confrontation. This militancy led to one of the biggest triumphs in the labour movement's recent history. This, in turn, contributed to the fact that the right wings of both the National Union of Mine-Workers and the Transport and General Workers' Union became a minority faction. One of the signatories of a pamphlet issued by regional NUM secretaries (1970, see Allen 1981) was elevated to a national figure during the 1972–1974 and 1984–85 miners' strikes. He is a Marxist and a member of the Labour Party. His name is Arthur Scargill. In 1981 he was overwhelmingly elected President of the National Union of Mineworkers. The retiring President Joe Gormley had previously attempted, by various manoeuvres, to keep this, the highest position in the NUM, from the reach of the union's left wing. When it became apparent during the late 1970s that the Communist Vice President of the NUM, Mick McGahey, might get the necessary votes to become President of the NUM, Joe Gormley decided to stay in office beyond his time. In 1980 McGahey would be fifty-five years old and hence, according to the constitution of the NUM, ineligible for the office of NUM President. Ultimately, these tactics were to no avail, as the union's left wing chose Arthur Scargill who was only forty-three when he took office in 1981; his relative youth therefore meant that he would be able to direct NUM affairs even longer than Mick McGahey would have been able.

The 1972 miners' strike achieved a degree of mobilization of other unions as well as of large sections of public opinion unknown since the General Strike of 1926. Previous union actions in response to the 1971 Industrial Relations Act, passed under the Heath Government, had already created some understanding of the more general political dimension of the dispute. In 1926 the miners remained largely isolated with their demands, and students were active strike-breakers as well as militiamen. In 1972 the demands put forward by the miners were broadly supported, although the intensive agitation of people like Arthur Scargill and Mick McGahey should not be forgotten. This time students staged demonstrations in solidarity with the miners, collected money for the strike and organized accommodation in students' halls of residences for flying pickets, sometimes even against the protest of the university administration as in the case of Essex University. Other unions supported the miners, too. There was no difficulty for the miners in ensuring complete cessation of coal production. One problem, however, was the huge pithead stocks which could have been used for a continuing supply to industry. The train drivers' union ASLEF immediately declared its solidarity with the miners, and a single picket sufficed to stop train drivers attempting to gain access to the coal stocks. The truck drivers, however, were employees of small companies or were specifically employed as strike-breakers or were not unionized. Hence mass picketing was needed to physically prevent truck drivers from getting through to stocks, thereby also demonstrating the serious nature of this strike. Mass picketing made it impossible for the police to keep gates open. During the second month of the strike, from 7 February to 10 February 1972, the biggest confrontation of the entire strike took place in front of the gates of the coal depot belonging to the Saltley Gasworks near Birmingham. This confrontation became symbolic of overwhelming solidarity and successful tactics in the history of the British trade union movement. It clearly showed that during the escalation of a strike, any confrontation can become a trial of strength and that a single decisive victory may completely turn the tide in favour of the workers. Saltley depot contained 100,000 tons of coal, and trucks from all over the country queued to transport it. 200 pickets were insufficient to stop this. Hence on Monday, 7 February, 1,000 flying pickets were drawn together. They were faced by 500 policemen. V.L. Allen writes in his history of the miners' union *The Militancy of British Miners*, how the confrontation developed over the following days:

The Saltley depot became the centre of a symbolic struggle. The coke which was being distributed from there had virtually no effect on the total power situation; it could not alleviate the increasing difficulties being confronted by industry. Nonetheless it represented a trial of strength which each side felt it had to win. The national office of the NUM appealed for all available pickets to go to Saltley. The secretary of the Birmingham Trades Council also appealed for pickets to assist the miners. On Tuesday, 8th February 1800 Midland car delivery workers struck in sympathy with the miners and on the following day about 200 shop stewards in the Midland engineering industry called for a solidarity stoppage by 40,000 engineering workers and a march to Saltley on Thursday, 10th February. The West Birmingham district secretary of the Amalgamaged Union of Engineering and Foundry Workers, Mr. Norman Cartwright, expressed the feelings of the shop stewards when he said that, 'This plant will be closed until the West Midland Gas Board accepts the conditions laid down by the miners union— that coke can only go to essential users. If any lorries from our well-organized factories try to cross the picket lines tomorrow, they can forget about coming to those factories in future. . .'

There was a coincidence of events as the confrontation at Saltley came to a head. The State of Emergency had been declared. Power cuts were enforced throughout the country affecting about one-third of the domestic, commercial and industrial users of electricity. There were unpredictable blackouts. Industrial workers were being laid off or put on short-time in increasing numbers. The British Steel Corporation, Courtaulds and Tate and Lyle in particular were affected. There was talk in Parliament about using troops.

Thursday, 10th February, was the day of mass action in Saltley. Almost 40,000 workers in the Birmingham area went on strike and 10,000 of them marched to Saltley to join the 2000 miners who were already there from South Wales, Yorkshire and the central coalfields. This was mass picketing on such a massive scale that the 1000 police on duty were insufficient to control the situation in the interests of the coke consumers. The Chief Constable of Birmingham ordered the gates of the Saltley depot to be closed.

(Allen, 1981, pp. 198–9.)

This miners' victory has entered the annals of the British trade union movement as the 'battle of Saltley'. This successful episode of union readiness to fight is also interesting with regard to reports by the press. Their ideological and political biases create a 'closed world' which is artificial as well as blind towards the signs of the time. Even the *Daily Mirror*, which portrays itself as a Labour daily, wrote at the beginning of the strike: 'The coming coal strike billed for Sunday is the saddest industrial cock-up since the war. Rarely have strikers advanced to the barricades with less enthusiasm or hope of success. . .'

(Allen, 1981, p. 207.)

Two years later, in 1974, the Heath Government clearly underrated the strength of fighting spirit of the miners and became the victim of its own porpaganda, which alleged that only a handful of agitators like Mick McGahey and Arthur Scargill were responsible for the miners' demands. The Government again acted intransigently, thought the miners to be isolated and fought an early general election with the slogan 'Who Governs Britain? The Unions or the democratically elected Government?' Edward Heath lost both general elections in 1974, held in February and October of that year. Margaret Thatcher succeeded him in 1975 as leader of the Conservative Party. The New Right in the Tory Party had taken control. In 1979 a different government, James Callaghan's Labour Government, was defeated at the polls after union demands had been ignored and the political mood in the country wrongly assessed. The 1984–85 miners' strike was fought in a political terrain that had been dramatically transformed. It was one of the most protracted disputes in the nation's history. In the absence of a national ballot being held, and in the presence of mass-picketing and mass-policing, it divided the country as well as the miners. After one year of enormous sacrifice, striking miners went back to work without agreement. Working miners, particularly in the Nottinghamshire coalfield, decided by ballot to proceed with the formation of the breakaway Union of Democratic Mineworkers (UDM) towards the end of 1985.

THE RIGHT TO INEQUALITY: THE CONSERVATIVE PHILOSOPHY OF THE 1980s

What is the situation in the 1980s? Will the trade unions be able to keep their positions or will their power be broken decisively? Industrial disputes since Thatcher's Conservative Government came to power (1979), for example in the coal, steel, car and railway industries as well as in the National Health Service, have not been successful in altering government policies towards working people. The reason for the low fighting spirits of workers cannot just be sought in lack of organization or decreasing 'politization'. The entire mood has changed. Optimism regarding a society of full employment and economic prosperity has given way to the pessimism of a stagnating nation which does not have a recipe for coping with her increasing problems. Towards the end of the 1970s a mood of lethargy spread, it was expected that the situation would get worse, and several million unemployed people appeared to be the inevitable consequence of general economic decline rather than of specific government policies.

Right until the end of the 1960s, public opinion was dominated by the achievements of reconstruction, especially after the privations of the war years. 'The West has never had it so good. For twenty years the industrial nations have been on a rising tide of material wealth', reads a quotation from *History of the 20th Century* published in (1969), edited by the well respected historian A.J.P. Taylor. Only ten years later, public opinion had gone to the other extreme, probably as exaggerated as the previous deception, and journalists, politicians and scientists all seemed to engage in sombre prognoses. A big conference on the problems of the 1980s, attended by politicians as well as academic experts, took place in 1979 under the title 'Is Britain dying?' The myth of a threatening apocalypse is substituted for the legend of the affluent society. This change in myths involves a series of revisions in the nation's conception of herself.

One of the most far-reaching corrections affected the public's picture of workers. In the *History of the 20th Century* there are references of the 'worker as king' during the first two post-war decades. For the first time in the history of capitalism, the wages of industrial workers had reached the level of those of white-collar workers. The National Health Service reduced the financial burden on many working class families considerably, and the hire-purchase system enabled them to acquire consumer goods which had previously been confined to the middle and upper classes. The traditional class barriers seemed broken. Researchers like John H. Goldthorpe concluded in a 1968 study that 'affluent workers', the modern avant-garde of the working class, had broken with the class consciousness of their fathers and aspired to acquire material wealth just like the middle classes. The new type of worker could be seen as a consumer of wares which had hitherto been regarded as luxury goods, like the car, the refrigerator, the television as well as holidays abroad. This new type of worker seemed to be integrated, content, bourgeois. It is quite revealing that the middle classes have corrected this image of the gradual merger of the classes during the repercussions of the 1970s. Today, they re-emphasize the 'right to inequality', as it is phrased in the language of the New Right.

In 1979, Sir Keith Joseph (who retired from the Government on 21 May 1986 after four years as Secretary of State for Education and Science) published a polemical pamphlet against 'socialist egalitarianism'. His work is entitled simply *Equality* and was meant to represent a refutation of social historian R. H. Tawney's book of the same title (published 1931). Tawney's writings were very influential with many leading politicians of the Labour Party (as well as with some of the leading figures of the newly founded Social Democratic Party). Sir Keith Joseph was educated at Harrow Public School and at Magdalen College Oxford. He practised law at the Middle Temple, is a board member of an international investment company and has been a member of several Conservative cabinets since 1962. His book contains blunt affirmations for the maintenance of class privileges. The question of personal wealth and the problem of class divisions are regarded as entirely unconnected phenomena by Sir Keith. Class divisions have much more to do with cultural rather than economic differences, he contends. Sir Keith's real intention, however, is to deliver a convincing justification as to why private acquisiton of wealth is perfectly legitimate and is not an unjust accumulation of surplus value which is then lost for society. Sir Keith concedes that personal enrichment may carry certain dangers but he sees these only as threatening the person himself. 'Private wealth like political power may corrupt, but unlike political power its corruption does not harm others.' (Joseph, 1979, p. 53.) He then lists at great length examples of people who managed to rise from the poverty of the working class to the wealth and privileges of the establishment. He concludes that the different capabilities of people will again and again produce inequalities in wealth. He adds an assessment of those who still criticize his analysis:

It is not enough to say that the Chairman of ICI or Mr David Frost or the Duke of Norfolk has too much and ought to have less. For unless the person who says so can tell us how much less these gentlemen ought to have and on what basis their income ought properly to be calculated, we are entitled to assume that there is in reality no basis at all on which their income can be described as 'unfair' other than personal animosity and resentment, fed by envy.

(Joseph, 1979, p. 68.)

This kind of refutation of the philosophy of equality is nothing new, and like others before him Sir Keith Joseph tends to treat the problem of privilege and disadvantage as if it were a question of *individual* privileges and disadvantaged *individuals*. The stories of poor capitalists and land owners whose burden of taxation becomes ever greater may stir people with similar ideas to Sir Keith's, but they have indeed little to do with the worries of a worker's family. Hence, this anti-egalitarian propaganda is of interest not so much for its content as for its timing. This new pronouncement had been formulated with the help of Oxford historian Jonathan Sumption. When, after a decade of intense industrial disputes, a strengthening of the trade union movement and deepening economic crisis, inequality is again affirmed as being a natural phenomenon, then this indicates a fundamental change in the thinking of the ruling classes. Social equality is no longer the aim, even in theory, because the New Right feels that consensus policies have promoted the phenomenon of 'creeping Socialism', as it is derogatively called. The New Right is also highly conscious of what is at stake since the turn-around in economic development. The defeat of the Labour Party at two successive general elections (1979 and 1983) is in itself no guarantee that the objective of public ownership or socialization (control of economic activity by central and local government) can be stopped and reversed. Far greater efforts are necessary, including in the area of ideology.

Those institutions which developed out of socialist tendencies in the service sector as well as in local govern-ment have become an established part of our society, and their abolition would be resisted even by people who are right-wing in a party political sense. This is one obstacle for the Conservatives as they set out to carry out these policies. A second obstacle consists of the invisible relative strengths between the social classes. For example, Edward Heath's Government discovered that its 1971 Industrial Relations Act remained a dead letter because employers preferred to settle violations of this law by the unions out of court. Margaret Thatcher's Government may face similar difficulties over 'secondary picketing', which was made illegal. Her Government will furthermore be judged with the success or failure of the very comprehensive privatiza-tion programmes designed to 'beat socialism' once and for all. It will be interesting to survey and assess the policy of radical privatization at the end of Mrs Thatcher's period of government.

There is one area, however, where supporters of a publicly run organization have been more powerful than expected. This area is the National Health Service. After an initial boom of private health insurances between 1979 and 1981 the demand now stagnates and a comprehensive plan for additional hospital facilities all over the country had to be abandoned. Private health care in Great Britain offers for the majority of the privately insured only limited services such as uncomplicated routine operations, and both the general practitioner and the dentist remain excluded from private insurance. Hence what private health insurance offers is frequently confined to conveniences like a single hospital room and personal medical attention *within* the National Health Service. Privatization therefore does not mean the creation of an alternative health care system, but the separation of the profitable areas from the unprofitable ones. This will ultimately lead to a yet greater burden on the state, because it is the state which will continue to sustain financially the expensive infrastructure, whereas the financial fruits will be harvested by the private sector. This pattern is repeated in areas such as communication and transport where, for instance, profitable airline routes are to be opened to private companies while smaller unprofitable routes remain entirely within the public sector. Similar plans have been drawn up for bus services, under the euphemistic heading 'de-regulation'. A transport bill has been introduced to Parliament to this effect.

Privatization of parts of the Health Service is in all probability not going to be carried through quite as smoothly as planned by the Thatcher Government. When her Government set out to abolish the local Community Health Councils, which exercise some democratic control of the National Health Service, the Government met the resistance of the British Medical Association, which is in principle well disposed towards Conservative governments. The Community Health Councils remained. This contradiction between a general political attitude, which may be rather conservative, and a particular stand on a particular issue, which may be much less conservative, seems to suggest that the decline of electoral support for the British Labour Party may not at all be an expression of a genuine swing to the right among the electorate. In actual praxis many people today defend 'socialist' achievements without being, in their ideological conception of themselves, at all well disposed towards socialist ideas in general.

THE FORWARD MARCH OF LABOUR HALTED?

What is the response of the British labour movement to these political developments? Has it lost the historic initiative needed to meet the challenge? Marxist historian Eric Hobsbawm initiated a debate in 1978 which has lasted to this day. He formulated the thesis that although the crisis of British capitalism had deepened, the labour movement had not succeeded in gaining strength according-ly. Industrial disputes are increasingly solely about money and serve particular interests. *The forward march of Labour Halted?*, was Hobsbawm's initial question. Has a century-long forward march really come to a halt? Hobsbawm himself seemed to say 'yes' to this question. Unionists, politicians, publicists have debated Hobsbawm's thesis, but most of them disagreed with him. There appears to be a certain amount of perplexity as to the inter-pretation of contradictory tendencies within the British labour movement. The most pronounced argument against Eric Hobsbawm's thesis is provided by Ken Gill, a Com-munist member of the executive of the Trade Union Congress (TUC) and General Secretary of the metalworkers union AUEW-TASS. Ken Gill writes:

The historic task facing our movement is to establish the working class as the leading force in British society. Recent history shows that, far from the 'forward march of labour' being halted, substantial advances have been made along this road. Organized labour is now a political power in the land and therefore the main enemy of the rulers of Britain; it cannot be swept aside as it was between the wars.

(Hobsbawm, 1981, p. 23.)

During the summer of 1981 Eric Hobsbawm put together a preliminary postscript to this debate. He retained his analytical assessment and warned against over-estimating Labour's swing to the left. As Hobsbawm sees it, the key question will be whether the Labour Party succeeds in getting sufficient support for a socialist programme among the general population: 'The future of Labour and the advance to socialism depends on mobilising people who remember the date of the Beatles' break-up and not the date of the Saltley pickets. . .' (Hobsbawm, 1981, p. 181.)

The secession of the social democratic forces from the Labour Party and their formation into an independent Social Democratic Party (SDP) was not a positive development for Labour, because the support of people represented by the SDP is absolutely indispensable for the realization of a socialist programme. Hobsbawm concludes from British post-war history to date that a good programme for a socialist society is necessary, but there is little hope of winning the support of the electorate for such a programme. Most people vote for one party (rather than another) more on the basis of a vague hope of change in a particular direction rather than for a concrete programme. Socialist ideas had to be communicated in the light of the social, cultural and economic change which Great Britain has undergone since 1945: 'The case for socialism is as strong as ever, but it has to be argued in a new way, with much clearer proposals concerning the sort of society we want and what socialism can achieve, rather than a repetition of old slogans which, however valid, no longer carry the same conviction.' (Hobsbawm, 1981, p. 177.)

Is the current passiveness of the labour movement a sign of stagnation? Why does the labour movement stand in front of the gates of power without having the keys to gain entry? Why are the forces of the status quo still so strong?

The question why Britain has not experienced any violent revolutions since the industrial revolution, despite a series of historical opportunities, is illuminating for understanding British history. Journalist and writer G.K. Chesterton remarked succinctly: 'The most important event in England in the nineteenth century was the revolution that did not occur.'

Young German writer Georg Weerth was employed in 1843 in the Bradford branch of a German trading company. He familiarized his friend Friedrich Engels in nearby Manchester with the social revolutionary ideas of the Chartists. Weerth wrote enthusiastically to his brother in 1844: 'Socialist ideas proliferate in England in an astonishing way. We only need crop failures for two successive years and some mishap in the world of commerce, and the revolution will be perfect' (translated from Weerth, 1974, Vol. I, p. vii).

However, revolutions were only witnessed on the European Continent, and not in Britain itself. The Chartist movement subsided. Britain subsequently experienced *many riots but no revolution.* It is astonishing that there should be such a contradiction between the militancy and the sacrifices of workers and employees such as manifested themselves during the 1978–79 'winter of discontent' as well as during the 1984–85 Miners' Strike and the rather insignificant social and political changes resulting from these disputes. Britain's national history has shown unique continuity. Parallelling this, the labour movement has clung to the organizational forms and procedures which it has established. One example of this is the organizational continuance of some autonomous unions in branches of industry which have ceased to exist. Who would dare to reform structures in one area if all other institutions stay as they are? The vacuum created by the dissolution of the old structures could be exploited by a political opponent.

LIVING TRADITION: THE WORKING MEN'S CLUBS

The peculiar combination of modern life style and obsolete structures finds its expression in the everyday lives of workers, too. The so-called working men's clubs are an excellent example. They are leisure time associations, more than a hundred years old. Today they are often quite modern entertainment centres, without having lost the character of private members' clubs of working class people. Contrary to the gentlemen's clubs they are much more numerous and distributed all over the country. The most lively working men's clubs may be found in the northern industrial areas or in the South of Wales. There are more than 3,500 registered working men's clubs and the total membership is more than three million people.

The history of these clubs mirrors to some extent the history of British working class culture. They began around 1860 on the initiative of the churches. The first clubs were paternalistic creations of factory owners and land owners. Rich factory owners gave money towards this purpose in order to combat drinking in public houses. They conceived a workers' club as some kind of moral institution of the people. In 1874, The Club and Institute Union, the parent organization of the working men's clubs which is still in existence today, listed eleven dukes as vice presidents, in addition to the Prince of Wales, numerous earls, barons and MPs. The workers, however, rapidly made themselves independent, and new clubs were founded in many back-rooms and houses. They assembled furniture and carried out redecorations by themselves. The aristocrats soon retired when it became clear that they had lost control over the movement. Abstinence was soon abandoned. During the 1880s, the working men's clubs became centres of political radicalism. At that time, one of the biggest and most famous working men's clubs was the Boro' of Hackney Club. Club life consisted of regular lectures and courses. On political demonstrations the club band would play music and the club banner would be proudly carried. Clubs also had their *clubman*, whose satirical description reveals a little of the sunday-like atmosphere in the club.

He goes to the club in the morning about 11, sits with a pot in front of him, and froths at the mouth over all sorts of socialist rot; then he has a band which finishes up by playing the Marseillaise; in the afternoon he goes round and visits other clubs and then is more frothy at the mouth and of the pot.   (Taylor, 1972, p. 46.)

From about 1890 onwards, however, the character of club life changed. Lectures became rarer, politics eliminated and light entertainment featured predominantly. A report in 1892 in the *Club and Institute Journal* concludes:

The entertainment manager becomes the most important official of the club, for he knows the power he has of attracting hundreds of members belonging to the club and affiliated to it. The political secretary and the manager of the evening classes are looked upon as superfluous, and rather encumbrances than any assistance.

(Taylor, 1972, p. 60.)

The working men's clubs have retained the character of a sociable meeting place as well as an entertainment centre to this day. During the 1960s many clubs implemented costly modernization. Concert halls with large stages, spotlights and comfortable seats were built and national and international showbusiness stars, ballet companies and comedians give performances. Are they still working men's clubs? Without a doubt. Most of them not only continue to carry the title working men's club, but these are also located in working class areas. Both guests and members are workers and their families and they administer the clubs themselves. Martin Leighton describes a visit to one of these modern clubs in his book *Men at Work*. The club, situated in the mining town of Ashington, in the north, clearly appears to be the cultural focus of this small town:

Some of them in Ashington are on an impressively large scale, with several bars and lounges, dance floors, snooker rooms, assembly halls, and facilities for all sorts of indoor games. The Comrades (the name is not intended to be political) is one of the grandest, and has a *weekly* turnover of £7500, which is in itself a comment on the management efficiency of its committee of miners. No evening is without some special entertainment—a cabaret, a dance, bingo, competitions and shows—the members collared and tied, their wives in party dresses, the bars crowded and the barmen run off their feet. Many of them started with more serious intentions, as places for evening classes and discussion, and most of them had libraries. These have largely disappeared with the new prosperity; women are allowed membership in their own right, and, though the strictest standards of behaviour are enforced, the mood is frankly sybaritic. At the same time, all of them take very seriously the support of local charities like the hospital, the blind, or the elderly, and, in addition, run Christmas clubs, funeral clubs, clothing clubs— echoes from their past of common financial hardship when what you might call socialised thrift made possible a festive turkey or a decent burial.

Most people in the town belong to several clubs, so they are neither competing with each other nor could it be claimed that they create socially divisive cliques. At root, though, they are run for working men and by working men, and in this respect exclusive.

(Leighton, 1981, p. 23.)

The aristocratic or middle class gentleman is proud that his own club still looks and functions as it did 100 years ago. The worker is proud of modernization and change in his club. Today's gentleman imitates the affectations of an epoch long since past. The worker remembers the same past as oppressive and exploitative. He is delighted that his time as a poor proletarian should now be part of the past. The past means something completely different for one person than for another. Does it follow that the ruling classes are characterized by romantic and reactionary memories and the working class by future-oriented optimism? Hardly.

Public consciousness is still dominated by the country's colonial past and by the myth of the glorious Empire. The people's democratic tradition remains buried or, worse, becomes incorporated in Imperial British ideas, thereby robbed of all revolutionary content. One example of this is William Blake's revolutionary confession:

> I will not cease from mental fight,
> Nor shall my sword sleep in my hand,
> Till we have built Jerusalem
> In England's green and pleasant land.

The Jerusalem for which William Blake fought under a religious pretext, is a classless society of free people. The word Jerusalem contains the connotation of emancipation and dissolution of all social classes for the British labour movement (hence, in this context, the meaning of the word Jerusalem is separated from its Christian and Jewish content). In this sense, John Gorman's aforementioned collection of workers' photographs bears the title *To Build Jerusalem*. Every year, William Blake's poetic lines cited above are sung by thousands of people during the Proms in the Royal Albert Hall in London. The song belongs to the canon of unofficial national anthems of Britain. Many may sing it without ever realizing its secular, revolutionary meaning. During the Proms it is usually played together with the nationalist song *Rule Britannia! Britannia rule the waves*, which juxtaposes Jerusalem with a different tradition altogether, thereby jeopardizing its original meaning. The emancipatory and Imperial traditions are hence pressed into the same framework. Within this obsolete social framework, where might the path of the working class lead it—before the framework itself is broken. Is it with this objective in view that Eric Hobsbawm talks about the *Forward march of Labour halted?*

CHAPTER FOUR

Blacks
and the
unsurmounted colonial past

'COLONIZATION IN REVERSE'

To this day, Great Britain has not developed a critical attitude to the country's colonial past. She simply has not come to terms with it. The complacent colonial doctrine continues to live on in public opinion, which sees colonization as an act of civilization, which not only pacified underdeveloped peoples but also brought modern public administration and technology to them. Although the shadowy side of the British Empire has been documented and researched, such research did not succeed in penetrating the public domain. During the Falklands War, all Westminster parliamentary parties agreed that the issue of the Falkland Islands represented neither a colonial conflict nor was it reminiscent of the colonial past. The official attitude to Britain's colonial history is usually limited to a quotation of the fact that the United Kingdom has granted independence to the vast majority of its colonial territories overseas. Today, what counts is the Commonwealth which is composed of nations which enjoy both equal rights and full sovereignty. Apart from this, the official attitude is one which seeks to have nothing to do with the consequences of 400 years of colonial history. These consequences are global, involving entire societies and many personal tragedies; they will determine the future course of world history for some time to come. The peoples concerned, 'silent' for centuries, have only just begun to lay claim to their rights and demand restitution.

Understanding colonialism does not simply mean coming to terms with past deeds. It is much more important that the European societies which were and are involved in colonization come to comprehend the present-day consequences of their past expansionism. Indeed, colonization was so far-reaching that there is hardly a country in the world today which has not been gripped by it, either as ruler or as ruled. The key to understanding mankind's modern history lies in understanding the history of colonial oppression. The history of nearly every nation state can only be written if the colonial dimension is taken into account.

This dimension may well rebound on European societies. This is because a dramatic reversal of the original colonial expansion has taken place since the historic turning point of the early 1960s when most colonized peoples gained independence. The reversal is particularly noticeable in the two main colonial powers: Britain and France. Whereas for centuries the metropoles of colonial power destroyed and displaced foreign forms of government, and created overseas numerous white settlements which ruthlessly imposed their culture and language onto the indigenous population, France and Britain today have been made forcibly aware what it means to share their countries with people from foreign cultures and different ethnic origins. Of course, the immigration of Caribbean and African blacks as well as of Indians, Pakistanis and East Asians does not compare with the original British colonial domination. However, even the peaceful nature and comparatively small scale of this immigration is being resisted by drastic legislation and by official campaigns which represent immigration as a calamity endangering national integrity.

Jamaican poet Louise Bennett described in a satirical poem the migratory movements of West Indians in the 1950s as 'colonization in reverse'. Her Jamaican dialect poetry suggest a wry smile at this historical reversal:

> What a joyful news, miss Mattie,
> I feel like me heart gwine burs'
> Jamaica people colonizin'
> Englan in reverse.
>
> An week by week dem shippin off
> Dem countrymen like fire,
> Fe immigrate and populate
> De seat o' de Empire.

(English Centre, p. 16.)

Of course, the actual existence of 'colonization in reverse' is out of the question. The poem cited here dreams jokingly of clandestine revenge by the colonized. By referring to such utopian dreams, the poem rather points to the unsaid, real situation which generates the dream of counter-colonization. The reality of the present still shares many of the features of past colonization. The United Kingdom aimed at terminating colonialism by signing declarations of independence, as if thereby she could relieve herself of all human and social consequences originating from her colonial activities. The human wreckage of colonialism would cease to be a British business, despite centuries of indoctrination which talked of Britain as the 'mother country'. If one is referring to aspects of neo-colonization, then the 'colonization of the mind' must surely be included: in particular, the loss of one's own, native language and the repudiation of one's own culture. It is this process of brain-washing, in which so many peoples were compelled to undergo this long period of 'colonial reorientation' which makes it so very difficult for these very peoples to find adequate ways of national renewal and continuity. Europe remains the model: the colonized peoples not only learnt to express their thoughts in European languages, they also learnt to forget the exploration and development of their own histories, languages and cultures. This is exemplified in the history of blacks in both Americas and the Caribbean. They represent descendants of slaves who were deported from Africa by the millions in order to cultivate colonial plantations, thereby generating enormous wealth for the colonialists. Slavery set forth the most brutal version of colonial exploitation. The resulting depopulation of vast African areas prohibited the organic development of many African societies. Kidnapping and plunder led to the decay of many African cultures. European civilization actually promoted cultural regression of these societies by further-ing the decay of traditional tribal organization as well as by increasing linguistic fragmentation. To the extent that Europeans exported their own cultures they helped to degenerate the indigenous ones.

This connection between culture and barbarity is a product of European expansionism and is *not* a natural result of different rates of social development. The civiliza-tion and progress of some peoples were paid for by barbarization and regression of others. The educated owner of a plantation, whose manor house not only contained a piano but also the latest books from Europe, co-existed with a black slave, who was not allowed to learn properly how to read, write or even talk, and who furthermore had to live in a shanty and whose physical strength was exploited to such an extent that he aged and died prematurely. The families of slaves were separated by force in order to prevent the development of com-munity solidarity. This principle even included the separation of babies from their mothers. When slaves were sold, it was strictly borne in mind that slaves belonging to the same cultural or linguistic sphere should never live together. The result was a disastrous cultural regression of many human communities whose members were forced to co-exist like animals, and who could communicate with each other only by making use of a truncated English vocabulary as they were unable to understand each other's native African tongue. This systematic barbarization created the precondition for the merciless exploitation of the colonized as 'work horses'. The enslavement taking place at the peripheries of the Empire coincided with the development of parliamentary democracy in the metropolis (mother country). As with classical Greece, where democracy of the few went hand in hand with the enslavement of the many, humanism and democracy in eighteenth century Europe developed in the shadow of imperial colonial barbarity. When today people seek to identify an unbroken parliamentary tradition in which colonial crimes are understood as the excesses of an otherwise humane system of government, then history is just as much being falsified as when the industrial revolution is presented as primarily a period of pioneering achievements in the area of technology.

Aimé Césaire, poet and politician of Martinique, an island which remains French to this day, wrote his famous essay *Discours sur le Colonialisme* (1955), in which he accused Europe of having undermined its humanist tradition by the pursuit of a dehumanizing colonization. No-one brutalizes another without at the same time brutalizing himself, argues Césaire. The barbarity in Nazi Germany was not an exception, but the consequence of the moral degeneration and disruption of Europe, initiated by colonialism and immensely worsened by the fact that the crime of colonialism was continually legitimized, sublimated and repressed by philosophers, writers, scientists and politicians. Césaire writes (1973, p. 13): 'Au bout de l'humanisme formel et du renoncement philosophique il y a Hitler.' (At the end of the road of formal humanism and philosophical abdication there is a Hitler.)

He continues that inside every Christian, humanistic, bourgeois European resides a Hitler, who remains concealed from him. As is true for every Afro-Caribbean person in the West Indies or Antilles, Aimé Césaire is a descendant of slaves. His native African tongue, culture and origins are unknown to him; he was educated in French culture, as if he were living in Poitiers or Lille, as if slavery had never happened and as if Africa had nothing to do with his own history. The obliteration of the past history of these African peoples was so complete that after twenty years of independence and self-administration little has changed regarding the eurocentrism of their cultural lives, and even less has changed regarding European economic dominance. Colonial injustice continues, though its form has altered considerably. For instance, Britain has brought up the descendants of slaves as 'little Englanders'. In the 1950s Britain also encouraged them to take up employment in the mother country, later she wished to rid herself of them, as if they were some foreign intruders who had nothing to do with the country. If one speaks of the colonial heritage, then these phenomena are part of the story.

HOMELAND JAMAICA

As in most former colonial territories, there is a pro-Western middle class in Jamaica whose social position is directly dependent on the connection with the West. In some instances their behaviour is more European than the Europeans. Since the amount of available resources is much less than in the West and since the discrepancy between the poor and the rich is much greater than it is in the West, there are much sharper class confrontations in Jamaica. Such social conditions are not conducive to compliance with democratic rules, nor should one expect them to be. Take the example of the People's National Party of Jamaica (PNP), a member of the Socialist International, which governed Jamaica until 1980 and maintained good relations with Cuba whilst in power. Although defeated at the polls in 1980, they cannot be said to have been truly defeated, because they became the victim of a destabilization campaign, inspired by the United States. Against the background of a very strenuous struggle for life, where the struggle for sheer physical survival inevitably takes precedence for most people, organized terror by armed political gangsters was sufficient to instigate the desired swing to the right at so-called

E

free elections.

A direct impression of this struggle for survival is given by the Jamaican film *The harder they come* (1972). Reggae singer Jimmy Cliff plays the lead part of a young man who has come from the ghetto and who wants 'his fair share':

> They say the world is spinning around
> They say the world is upside down
> They tell of the pie up in the sky
> Waiting for me when I die
> But between the day when you are born and when you die
> They never seem to hearing you cry
> So as shure as the sun will shine
> I'm going to get my share right now what's mine and then
> The harder they come the harder they fall, one and all.

Jamaican writer Michael Thelwell based a novel on the events in the film, which was published in 1980 under the same title. Written in Jamaican dialect, the book provides a good insight into the social and political situation of contemporary Jamaica. The character of the ghetto child in *The harder they come*, who wants to free himself from poverty and a hopeless future, by robbery and murder, represents an archetype of neo-colonialism. However, as the oppression is of a social nature, liberation from it can only succeed collectively. Countries like Jamaica are faced with the necessity of a radical break with their colonized pasts.

The middle classes and the educated have been the most strongly involved in European education. Therefore, they have the deepest perception of the connection. A revolutionary break with the colonial past would mean the destruction of the eurocentric identity and outlook of this leading stratum of society. The writer V.S. Naipaul, whose family, of Indian descent, belongs to the leading class of Trinidad, described this post-colonial situation from a sarcastic and cynical perspective: the West Indian as a clown without identity, living amidst the chaos of cultures originating from all parts of the world. Naipaul represents those Caribbean intellectuals, who readily analyze the present situation as untenable, but reject socialist transformation. Michael Thelwell, author of *The harder they come*, calls Naipaul a 'foreign correspondent of the Western Intelligentsia'. The former Jamaican Prime Minister and present leader of its socialist opposition, Michael Manley, is different. He clearly belongs to the progressive politicians of this Caribbean island, although still deeply rooted in the British education and tradition which have shaped his identity. In a commentary in the *Guardian* on the inner city riots during the spring and summer of 1981 in Great Britain, Manley writes about himself as the perfect example of an anglicized black:

By the time I was 14, I think I knew far more about Britain than about Jamaica. . . I did not know how Jamaica was governed because nobody had taught me; nobody had asked me and nobody seemed to think that it was worth knowing anyway!

I had a feel for the English countryside long before I ever saw it; a feeling that grew out of the pages of Wordsworth to be confirmed in the reproductions of Constable. Deep impressions of England, its way of life, its institutions. . .

We still struggle to regain a past that is lost somewhere in the mists of time and the seas of the Middle Passage.

For few of us, then, did Britain ever become finally the object of unalloyed hatred and rejection. We were taught that this was 'mother'. When we arrive on the scene we quickly learn that this was not ours but someone else's 'mother'.

No less significant is the fact that, for better or for worse, you are now governed through an imitation, more or less faithful, of the Mother of Parliaments. You have probably saddled yourself, for better or for worse, with the sort of disputatious and often irrelevant two party system through which you hope to contain oppression. Consequently, however, you have little hope of mobilising people to the sorts of massive, united and sustained efforts through which alone can most Third World countries hope to work their way out of poverty and into development.

(Michael Manley, the *Guardian*, 21 July 1981, p. 9.)

Everywhere in the world from the missionary schools of the Kenyan Highlands to the military training schools situated in India, to the slave chapels of the Caribbean, European religion, literature, languages and values were taught. Moreover, the European way of life was praised as the high point of human civilization. And now Europe resists when a tiny part of these people, who have undergone 'European acculteration', pursue a little bit of 'colonization in reverse'. Even today, many white people hold key positions in the former colonies in industry, administration and in the universities. They often control the flow of capital or the direction of investment, commonly write syllabuses for schools and universities and sometimes take decisions of national importance, decisions which could crucially affect the development of these young independent countries. But if a black person becomes a lawyer, teacher or mayor in the former mother country, this is not treated as a matter of course but denounced as a dangerous tendency. The United Kingdom has coerced a constitution onto Zimbabwe, in which a tiny white minority retains special rights both in parliament and in public administration. Why is the black minority in Britain refused similar special rights? The principle of protection for minorities may still be extended to the deployment of gunboats to come to the aid of white, loyal Britons, as the Falklands War has shown. There is, of course, no comparable protection of black minorities in Britain.

HISTORY OF BLACKS IN GREAT BRITAIN

Black settlers have been resident in Great Britain for several hundred years. From the very beginning, their presence was actively resisted by the state. Deportation is not an invention of our time. Even then it was viewed as an appropriate way to expel foreign settlers. A royal proclamation by Queen Elizabeth I in 1601 let it be known that the Lübeck merchant Caspar van Senden had been instructed to take 'negroes and blackamoors' resident in England out of the country. The proclamation justified the decision as follows:

Whereas the Queen's majesty, tendering the good and welfare of her own natural subjects, greatly distressed in these hard times of dearth, is highly discontented to understand the great number of Negroes and blackamoors which (as she is informed) are crept into this realm since the troubles between her highness and the King of Spain; who are fostered and relieved here, to the great annoyance of her own liege people who want the relief which these people consume, as also for that the most of them are infidels having no understanding of Christ or his Gospel: hath given especial commandment that the said kind of people shall be with all speed avoided and discharged out of this her majesty's dominions.   (File/Power, 1981, p. 6.)

However, the presence of blacks is testified to in later times as well, a fact which makes the success of the royal decree somewhat doubtful. For example, black musicians were said to be attractions for festive processions in the city of London.

Due to the expanding slave trade in the eighteenth century, the black population in Britain grew rapidly. Blacks entered the country mainly as slaves of the owners of colonial plantations, but also as sailors and servants who had bought their freedom. Advertisements for sales of slaves could be read in both English and American newspapers. America, of course, still formed part of the overseas territories of the English Crown. The following advertisement was published in 1709 in *Tatler*: 'A Black boy, twelve years of age, fit to wait on a gentleman, to be disposed of at Denis's Coffee House in Finch Lane, near the Royal Exchange.' (The *Tatler*, 1709.) (Communist Party, 1980, Unit I.)

Similar advertisements could regularly be found in all English newspapers and magazines next to offers of cloth, country estates, pets and small property. The advertisements were usually short, snappy and business-like, similar

to this one in the *Daily Ledger* of 1761: 'A healthy Negro
Girl aged about fifteen years; speaks English, works at her
needle, washes well, does household work, and has had
the smallpox.' (From *Daily Ledger*, December 31, 1761.)
(Communist Party, 1980, Unit I.) References to diseases
or physical disabilities were frequent.

Notices about runaway slaves were also published to an
increasing extent. Some must have been unsuccessful, as a
series of them appeared and they were reprinted at regular
intervals. The following announcement was published over
several months in *British Apollo*:

Runaway from his Maiter on the 14th Instant, one Tho. Jones,
about 24 Years of Age, with Pock-holes in his Face, a dark Brown
Wig, in a Grey Cloath Livery lin'd with black, Stammers a little in
his Speech, whoever brings him to Mr. Dikes, by the Horfe-fhooe
Tavern in Drury-lane, shall have two Guineas Reward.

(File/Power, 1981, p. 11.)

Runaway slaves undoubtedly escaped to the docklands
of the great cities of London, Liverpool or Bristol, where
a considerable number of black people had become
resident. We know little about their work, life or fate. It is
only the response of their white masters which has been
bequeathed to posterity in precise detail. An influential
journal of the time, *The Gentleman's Magazine*, contained
a commentary on 'the black danger' in 1764. The imperious
tone and outspoken nature of the language seems to throw
some light on the treatment of blacks in the colonies,
which was much more brutal than at home:

The practice of importing Negroe fervants into thefe kingdoms is
faid to be already a grievance that requires a remedy, and yet it is
every day encouraged, infomuch that the number in this metropolis
only, is fuppofed to be near 20,000, the main objections to their
importation is, that they ceafe to confider themfelves as flaves in
this free country, nor will they put up with an inequality of treatment, nor more willingly perform the laborious offices of fervitude
than our own people, and if put to do it, are generally fullen fpiteful,

treacherous, and revengeful. It is therefore highly impolitic to introduce them as fervants here, where that rigour and feverity is impracticable which is abfolutely neceffary to make them ufeful.

(File/Power, 1981, p. 1.)

The quoted figure of 20,000 negroes living in London is almost certainly grossly exaggerated, as the British capital only had approximately 650,000 inhabitants at the time. According to estimates today, the total black population in the United Kingdom during the eighteenth century did not exceed 10,000 to 15,000 people. After the American War of Independence, numerous black people, formerly slaves, entered the country. They had fought on the English side as they were promised freedom for this. In the eighteenth century, black people belonged to London's everyday life. In many distinguished circles it was considered smart to keep black servants. They were often fitted out with fantasy costumes in oriental-style and kept almost like exotic pets. Aristocratic ladies and gentlemen frequently ordered portraits with black people in their background, depicted in servile positions. Portraits of the Duchess of Portsmouth or of the Duke of Perth are good examples of this: the young slave of the Duke of Perth is wearing an iron collar, a cynical equivalent of the medieval armour of dukes.

One of the most descriptive sources on the role of the black in English society of that time is a series of paintings by William Hogarth. His satirical engravings and pictures *Marriage à la mode* depict blacks, quite unconventionally, in a rebellious, independent manner which makes one think of the notices of runaway slaves. In the painting *The rising of the Countess* (see figure 10), a bizarre company of would-be gentlemen are in attendance on a false countess. An Italian eunuch is singing an aria while the other visitors continue to drink cocoa and the 'countess' is indulging in delight. Everybody has been touched by William Hogarth's biting satire except the figure of the black servant. Georg Christoph Lichtenberg, who has examined Hogarth's engravings in detail, explicitly refers to the special treatment Hogarth gives black people:

Behind the delightful lady. . . we notice a head, or rather a head keeps staring at us, which is not one of the most beautiful, but one of the most telling of the entire society. It is a negroe's head, who seems to be serving hot chocolate into the blue. Well, with three diamonds in his face, one of which, on his nose, is both borrowed and bogus, he is outshining all the diamonds on the castrate's ear and solitary. Is that not language and meaning at the same time? And is it not Art to assign more meaning to the *symbol of new moon* on the African's shoulder than to the Italian *full moon*?

(translated from Lichtenberg, 1972, p. 957.)

Lichtenberg's observations are confirmed by additional engravings by William Hogarth. In *Mittag*, Hogarth juxtaposes a degenerate white dandy with a vigorous black person who is clapsing the breasts of a white maid. Ideas about the meaning of 'civilization' and 'barbarity' prevailing at that time are satirically confronted with each other in this picture. Hogarth scornfully exposes these ideas, as well as their symbols such as dress or colour, as being complacent prejudices. It is of particular interest that Hogarth's paintings represent black people as a self-evident part of English society—as selfish and human as itself. Hogarth's critical attitude, however, is exceptional among his contemporaries.

Institutionalized racism towards people of a different colour, who, after all, had not come of their own free will, had already become firmly entrenched in official ideology. The prevailing pattern of argument reveals astonishing parallels with arguments conducted in our time. The *Morning Post* of 29 December 1786 contained the following passage:

When so many of our own young men and women are out of employment, and, literally speaking, are starving in the streets, it is abominable that aliens, and more particularly Black aliens, should be suffered to eat the bread of idleness in Gentlemen's houses, &c.

(File/Power, 1981, p. 27.)

These hypocritical arguments against people whose lives had been wasted by displacement and by the hardest of labour served to legitimize a completely different matter, as expressed clearly and openly in *The Gentlemen's Magazine*. It was feared that blacks might become infected with ideas of freedom and independence. Precedents of this sort in the mother country could in turn endanger the British slave-holding society in the colonies. Civil rights activist Granville Sharp achieved judgements in a series of test cases which, although they did not declare slavery illegal, procured an important right by legally forbidding arbitrary acts of repatriation to overseas plantations. (The official abolition of slavery was enacted by Parliament in 1833.) The case of the slave James Somerset became famous. He had escaped his master and was to be deported to Jamaica after his recapture. James Somerset was set free by royal court order in 1772. Black people celebrated this sentence as a political victory. The *Public Advertiser* of 27 June 1772 contained the following news:

On Monday near 200 Blacks, with their Ladies, had an Entertainment at a Public-house in Westminster, to celebrate the Triumph which their Brother Somerset had obtained over Mr. Stuart his Master. Lord Mansfield's Health was echoed round the Room; and the Evening was concluded with a Ball. The Tickets for Admittance to this black Assembly were 5s. each.   (File/Power, 1981, p. 20.)

This report furthermore points to the autonomous social life which black people organized for themselves. We know from additional reports and from memoirs of educated blacks, such as Olaudah Equiano who travelled up and down the country around 1790 to campaign against slavery, that many blacks married white women and were able to lead independent lives in the society of their time. Nothing stood in the way of the development of peaceful coexistence of blacks and whites in what was then one of the richest countries of the world.

However, the slavery lobby fought back. Unable to

secure legal sanction, they employed other methods of deportation sanctioned by the state. The public mood was incited against the so-called 'black danger' and a picture of England was invoked which would soon be overpopulated by blacks. For instance, the *Morning Post* of 22 December 1786 cites a Mr Dunning, according to whom

the numerous dingy-coloured faces which crowded our streets, must have their origin in our wives being *terrified* when pregnant, by the numerous Africans who were to be seen in all parts of the town, and if the legislature did not take some method to prevent the introduction of any more, he would venture to prophecy, that London would, in another century, have the appearance of an Ethiopian colony. (File/Power, 1981, p. 27.)

Some men in public life found a method. A 'committee for the aid of poor blacks' was set up which in 1786 published a *Plan of a Settlement to be made near Sierra Leone, on the Grain Coast of Africa.* The public was asked not to give alms to poor blacks and every black beggar picked up in the street was given clothing and food only after he had signed disembarkation documents. Protest notes by Olaudah Equiano and by other black intellectuals like Ottobah Cugoano drew attention to the fact that the agents and captains responsible for the implementation of disembarkation misappropriated the finances provided for this purpose by crowding together their fellow black citizens like slaves. Furthermore, Olaudah Equiano underlined the hypocrisy of the whole enterprise of so-called free settlement in Sierra Leone. The coast of West Africa was full of trade posts run by slaveholders. If black people disembarked on the mainland without protection, they risked being caught by slaveholders who would once again put them without mercy on the road to slavery and misery. Additionally, many blacks originated from the Caribbean and were therefore completely unfamiliar with African climate, culture and way of life. Considering these circumstances, it is hardly surprising that despite coercion only a few hundred blacks could be found for settlement on the coast of Sierra Leone.

The contradictions of the eighteenth century- a century which developed the ideal of 'the gentleman'—are with us to this day. Every English schoolchild learns about the self-sacrificing life of Florence Nightingale. Her life story is told in numerous versions, as a shining example to the nation, and is honoured on bank notes issued by the Bank of England. Who has ever heard of the Creole Mary Seacole, however? Like Florence Nightingale, Mary Seacole nursed the ill and the wounded during the Crimean War. Her yellow dress, her blue cap and her bag of medicines were as known and famous on the battle-fields of Balaclava and Sebastopol as the torch of Florence Nightingale. Mary Seacole was born in Jamaica. She was experienced with tropical diseases and possessed a wide knowledge of medicinal herbs which her black mother had taught her. She had paid her own fare to the Crimean, and had come there against the wishes of the military leadership. Mary Seacole returned impoverished. Many grateful soldiers helped her, collecting money for her support during a four-day celebration. Mary Seacole was forgotten, whereas Florence Nightingale is not.

POLITICIANS, POLICE AND INNER-CITY RIOTS

To this day Europe is writing a selective history of the progressive development of her civilization. She would rather banish the ghosts which she herself has raised. Once again, leading British politicians talk about 'the black danger'. Before she became Prime Minister, Margaret Thatcher said publicly in 1978 that people were afraid Great Britain 'may become swamped by people of different culture'. The expression 'people of different culture' is insincere indeed, as only people of a different colour are meant and not immigrants from the continent of Europe. Also, the verb 'swamp' clearly shows subliminal resentment on the part of Mrs Thatcher, because as a noun the word 'swamp' also contains the meaning of marsh and morass. The 1981 police raid against the black inhabitants of Brixton was significantly termed *'Operation Swamp'*. This police raid was one of the factors sparking off the inner city riots of 1981. The term 'Operation Swamp' is reminiscent of the infamous fascist expression 'drainage of the swamp' which meant aggressive action against the opponents of fascist regimes. The use of metaphors of this sort to describe police action against people suggests that these people are enemies of the nation, against whom one was engaged in a legitimate war. Margaret Thatcher did not even feel inhibited about acknowledging the British neo-fascist movement National Front whose motto is 'For Race and Nation, against communism'. She declared in 1978: 'Some people do not agree with the objectives of the National Front, but they say that at least they are talking about some of the problems.'

Other politicians on the right surpass Mrs Thatcher in bluntness of language and in extremism of political purpose. The most important exponent of the contemporary variety of the idea of deportation for blacks is Enoch Powell, former Cambridge don of classical Greek and a former Conservative Cabinet Minister. In 1965 he was defeated by Edward Heath for the leadership of the Conservative Party. Enoch Powell, author of numerous nationalist writings and poetry, is today the Member of Parliament for Down (South), as candidate of the right-wing Official Ulster Unionist Party. Since the late 1960s, when he prophesied 'rivers of blood' between blacks and whites, Enoch Powell has propagated the idea of deportation of the entire coloured population of the United Kingdom. At various times, he has used expressions for deportation like 'repatriation', 'positive outflow', 're-emigration' or 're-settlement'. In 1976 he proposed a plan, whereby one million coloured people would be transported to Asia, Africa or the Caribbean, at a cost of £1,000 per person. This kind of deportation Powell termed 'real development aid':

Not only in financial terms but in the much more significant terms of human skills, experience and qualifications, the outlay would represent 'development aid' of a size and effectiveness which current expenditures on aid could not match; and in both human and material terms the future savings would be incalculable.

(Powell, *The Times*, 5 October 1976.)

During 1981, clashes broke out between the police and blacks in several British cities, and blood was shed. Again, Enoch Powell raised his voice and, in harmony with the mass media, misleadingly interpreted the unrest as 'race riots'. He said much worse was to come and the politicians who held responsibility were guilty of a 'conspiracy in silence'. Addressing Young Conservatives, Powell declared in March 1981: 'I see no reason to depart from the view I have long held and expressed, that at some point along the line of growth, absolute and proportionate, of the Commonwealth population in London and the other English cities affected there lies the certainty of violence on a scale which can only adequately be described as civil war.' (Powell, *The Observer*, 29 March 1981 and *Daily Telegraph*, 30 March 1981.)

Nowhere within the United Kingdom have blacks participated in clashes which had anything at all to do with what Powell called civil war. The riots were essentially conflicts with the police which degenerated into looting and street battles. They represented an outburst of resentment on the part of black youth who get into trouble with the police so frequently that one can speak of systematic persecution by the police. Nearly every black youngster has been questioned or searched by the police, or has been taken to a police station. A mere gathering of three or four blacks on the pavement arouses suspicion in the police. Not only are blacks harassed with questions, they often have to endure derogatory remarks. Hence they may easily arrive at the conviction that white society regards the colour of their skin as an offence or even a sign of criminality. Young blacks therefore grow up in a climate of conflict and even aggression. Quite often, policemen in civilian clothes stop black youngsters in the street who assume they are dealing with obstructive civilians and therefore pay back the abuse in the same coin. Before the plain-clothed policemen have properly proven their identity, it can come to blows, and the youngsters thereby become guilty of disrespect for public authority. But black adults are also increasingly complaining about being stopped and searched in their vehicles by the police without apparent reason, particularly if they are driving a new and expensive car. Incidents of this sort represent an uninterrupted chain of continuous harassment by the police. Policemen on the beat in predominantly black quarters are neither specially trained for duty there, nor are the authorities making much effort to recruit black policemen. In England and Wales, only 0.5 per cent of all policemen are in fact coloured. The witnesses to brutal encroachments by the police testify the crude racism of many policemen. A considerable number of the police regard black residential areas as hostile territory, and the only appropriate way to preserve law and order is to assert their authority with drastic measures. The Institute of Race Relations has presented hundreds of cases concerning all coloured communities from all parts of the country to the royal commission on the reform of criminal proceedings. The following quotation was taken from the magazine *Flame* and indicates the severity of conflict with the police:

In Peckham, in August 1976, the SPG arrested several young black people outisde a betting shop. The youths had noticed three or four men–who subsequently turned out to be plain clothes police–opposite. Fifteen minutes later they saw about 13 men coming down the road and, suspecting trouble, the youths went back in the shop. One of them was then called outside. He was grabbed, flung through the door and knocked down. He got onto his knees and, with his arms pinned behind his back, he was punched and kicked. Two girls, C.W. and D.W., were passing and C.W. (aged 13) thought her brother

was being attacked by a group of local white racists. She dashed
over the road and called out to ask if he were all right. She was
pushed by the police and told to 'piss off'. Two vans arrived, C.W.
was dragged in and hit in the van. Her hair was pulled and later at
the station she was stripped naked and searched, and also subjected
to verbal abuse. This 13-year-old was five foot two inches tall and
weighed seven stones. She was accused of assault on three SPG
officers.
(*Flame*, November 1976) (Institute for Race Relations, 1979, p. 32.)

For black youth the police are a perceptible barrier to
their living space in a society which has classified them as
an unwanted minority and has made the colour of their
skin a social stigma. Because of barriers put up by police
policy, other areas of society appear to be forbidden
territory. It seems as if the police push every protesting
black person back to his inner and outer ghetto. This is
one of the meanings for black people of 'institutionalized
racism'.

The inner city riots of 1981 were an escalation of
incidents, which had been caused by police raids. The
principle of 'appropriate means' was badly violated, and
the existing tension among black people was ignored. The
assessment of a black teenager, reported in the *Sunday
Telegraph* on 12 April 1981 after the first big wave of
conflicts had broken out, is valid for nearly all the clashes,
including those in Nottingham and in the Notting Hill area
of London which took place in 1958: 'It is not against the
white community, it's against the police. They have
treated us like dirt. Now they know it's not that easy.'
(*Sunday Telegraph*, 12.4.81) 'The reaction of the black
community was four square behind the youths.' (*Guardian*,
18.4.81).

The first riots were in April 1980 in the black quarter of
St Paul's in Bristol. For two hours the police had sealed
off a café which was a popular meeting point for black
teenagers. More and more people gathered together, and
when policemen led the owner of the café away in hand-
cuffs, stones and bottles were thrown at them. During the

ensuing, four-hour clash, 130 people were arrested, some of whom were taken to court for riotous behaviour. The punishment for such a misdemeanour may be up to several years' imprisonment. The court, which had four black jurors, decided that there was not sufficient proof. After several retrials all the defendants were set free. The mood was turning against such judgements as clashes of this sort came to be seen as a problem of the preservation of public order. Instead of pursuing the social causes of this smouldering conflict, the police force was urged by right-wing politicians, journalists and particularly by members of the security forces, not to give in to this kind of 'criminal behaviour and lack of discipline'. They were urged to nip the rebellion in the bud. This may have convinced some chief constables that the time was ripe for mass action to 'clean up' whole districts.

In this way, 'Operation Swamp 1981' was planned. The operation unleashed violent clashes in more than thirty British cities. The clashes took four months to die down and became known as 'inner-city riots'. During the period from 6 April to 11 April, Brixton saw the arrival of additional police forces which had been ordered to this part of London in order to stop and search all suspects every day between two o'clock in the afternoon and eleven o'clock at night. During the first four days 120 policemen in civilian clothing systematically combed the streets of Brixton; approximately 1,000 people were stopped and about 100 persons arrested. Very few of these 100 people were actually arrested for theft or burglery, which 'Operation Swamp' was officially supposed to deal with. Meanwhile, all Brixton had become aware of the fact that something special was going on. Nobody, how-ever, was informed of anything, rumours started going round and the feeling of being besieged began to spread. The level of nervousness was raised on both sides.

Then, on 10 April, the first street battles broke out. A minor incident sparked off the explosion of a riot. Just after six o'clock in the evening, police constable Margiotta, who was on the beat on Atlantic Road in the middle of Brixton, noticed a black youth running towards him, closely followed by other black adolescents. Supposing that this black person might be involved in some form of crime, the policeman started to follow him and grabbed hold of his arm. In so doing, the policeman realized that the teenager, whose name was Bailey, had a gaping wound and was covered with blood. As soon as the other teenagers had caught up with them, Bailey succeeded in breaking loose and ran away once more. In the meantime, an additional policeman had appeared and both policemen attempted to convince the growing crowd that they had no intention of arresting Bailey and that they wanted to take him in an ambulance to receive medical treatment. Bailey had meanwhile found refuge in a flat of some white people, whom he did not know, but who helped him to bandage his wound and then called a taxi for him. However, Bailey was recognized in the taxi by some policemen in a patrol car who stopped the taxi. A further patrol car appeared, and Bailey's wound was bandaged once again. Meanwhile, between forty and fifty teenagers had gathered, some shouting, 'They are killing him. Why don't they call an ambulance?' Some teenagers pulled Bailey out of the patrol car, exclaiming: 'We'll look after our own people!' They took Bailey along the road to ask somebody in a private car whether he would be able to take the injured person to the hospital. Approximately half an hour had elapsed since the beginning of this incident, and the whole affair could have been brought to a close at this point. The policemen, however, started to chase the teenagers and the first skirmish occurred. From the point of view of the police, the incident was a clear case of hindering the police in the execution of their duties, coupled with the suspicion of a criminal act.

However, a hardening of attitudes in addition to blindness towards the social dimension of the tensions were to increase even further during the course of the riots. The leader of *'Operation Swamp'* raised the number of patrol duties after this incident. On the following day, another comparatively harmless incident escalated into street battles at several sites in Brixton. For two consecutive days, the police and various crowds of between 200 and 300 people were engaged in fully fledged fights against each other. 172 civilians, 414 policemen and 14 firemen were injured. 28 houses were set on fire, 30 private cars and 4 patrol cars were destroyed and a further 118 damaged, in addition to a number of ambulances and fire brigade trucks.

As usual in times of crises, the British Parliament immediately attempted to calm the situation by setting up a public inquiry. One of the highest British judges, Lord Scarman, was appointed to head the commission of inquiry into the Brixton riots. When the Scarman commission took up its work in mid June, the events had become more and more critical. The riots had not remained confined to Brixton, but had spread to numerous English cities. And it became even worse. At the beginning of July, a group of skinheads (an extreme right-wing group of youngsters) attacked Asian shopkeepers in the Southall area of London. The week-end afterwards, severe street battles broke out in the Toxteth area of Liverpool. These battles were even more serious than those in Brixton. The Chief Constable of Merseyside, Kenneth Oxford, commented on these riots as follows: 'It is exclusively a crowd of black hooligans intent on making life unbearable and indulging in criminal activities.' (*The Guardian*, 6 July, 1981.)

Prime Minister Margaret Thatcher sanctioned this point of view, when she declared in Parliament in the same month: 'A large part of the problem which we are facing now results from the weakening of authority in many areas over many, many years. This will have to be corrected.' Since then, many different causes of these riots have been put forward, ranging from the disintegration of the structure of the family to the general lack of discipline in society. Many critics are undoubtedly right in pointing out the significance of the economic situation of black youth, who suffer a much higher rate of unemployment than their white counterparts and generally have worse career prospects.

The problem of police repression as a direct and localizable expression of institutionalized racism is central to the question of the immediate causes of the riots. The removal or alleviation of these immediate causes is possible within the existing framework. The official report of the Scarman commission (1981) clearly takes this problem into account by saying that the cause of the riots is found within a 'very complex social-political situation, which is not only applicable to Brixton'. The riots essentially represented 'an outbreak of fury and embitterment by young black people against the police'. However, the Scarman report confined his criticism to 'Operation Swamp', thereby not only depriving his statement of much of its significance, but also in fact denying the existence of a much more comprehensive form of institutionalized racism. Instead the report demands the abolition of discrimination on racial or ethnic grounds, as otherwise British society may well be threatened by destruction. Such a crude displacement of the problem of black Britons is as wrong as Enoch Powell's prophecy of civil war between black and white.

Today, nearly two million black people reside within the United Kingdom. In this context, the term black is understood politically and therefore includes all coloured residents originating from Africa, the Caribbean and the Indian sub-continent. It is widely assumed that in the year 2000 approximately three million black Britons will live in the UK, out of a total population of about 56 million. Black Britons of African origin account for about 800,000 to one million people. Social contacts between black and white people are generally much more harmonious than most media and some politicians would have us believe. There is no question—on either side- of collective racial resentment. The only peril comes from racist organizations and institutions with a racist orientation. These threaten to utilize the state and social apparatus for discrimination against ethnic minorities. This can be stopped, can be controlled, if an adequate political will exists. Racial hatred is not innate, it is incited. This is part of the legacy of colonialism. Oppression of people by others often goes hand in hand with contempt of oppressed people for themselves. Therefore, they fall victim twice. Racist organizations can be officially forbidden. Institution-alized racism can be similarly prohibited, like all other violations against human rights or the dignity of man. The myth of the 'friendly bobby' may make many whites blind towards the other side of the police, but the evidence for the repressive character of police and judiciary towards the black population is so overwhelming that it cannot be explained away as isolated incidents.

The course of events during the Brixton riots provides ample proof for this supposition. After the severe street battles of April were over, unrest in Brixton had nearly died down, when on 14 July the police again raided a part of Brixton in a manner which can only be understood as revenge. At about half past eleven at night, the residents of Brixton's Wiltshire Road were asked to remove their vehicles from the street. Soon afterwards, thirty police vehicles and personnel carriers drove into the road and subsequently barred it. Several land rovers equipped with dynamos for searchlights as well as dog patrols also appear-ed. At about half past one in the morning, the police convoy drove into nearby Railton Road, which had seen many of the violent clashes between people and police during the past few months. Railton Road, too, was sealed off and the police stormed—without any prior warning—houses 50 to 64, a café at 37 and a small warehouse. The action by the police clearly bore the character of a military conquest. Doors and windows of these houses were smashed with heavy hammers. The inhabitants were given absolutely no chance to grant permission for the search of their homes. The next day, a delegation of members of parliament and Lord Scarman himself came to see the destruction: doors had been chopped to pieces; plugs were pulled out and wiring torn apart; beds, arm-chairs and floors had been ripped open; furniture had been broken and radios and television sets demolished. The official explanation by the police was that this action had been initiated on the grounds of information, supplied by a source which had proved reliable in the past, that Molotow cocktails were to be found and alcohol was illegally dispensed. None were found. Out of a total of seven arrests, five were for illegal possession of drugs. The disproportionality of the means employed by the police was staggering, and the statement given by Chief Constable David Powis was cynical:

Unfortunately (sic) we did not find petrol bombs, but I am convinced that these devices existed at the time we received the information. We were bound to do what we did. . . we cannot claim the raid was an overwhelming success. But it is a real world when you're searching for these devices and that sometimes means damaging property.

(Anning, 1981, p. 10.)

The attitude of this Chief Constable is typical of leading officials of the security forces. For them the problem of black Britons is a question of the preservation of law and order, just as it has been formulated by the Conservative Government.

LINTON KWESI JOHNSON

The traumatic experience for the individual of a confrontation with the superior force of the police and the judiciary has been, from a literary point of view, handled most effectively by black writers. Linton Kwesi Johnson may be the most important poet of Britain's black people. He was born in Jamaica in 1952 and brought up in the country by his grandmother. He was deeply influenced by the local, oral tradition, a tradition which is largely passed on in the form of folk songs, ghost stories, work songs and riddles.

His mother took him to England in 1963. He has been living in Brixton since and is a member of the collective *Race Today*, which issues a journal of the same name. After initial attempts written in standard English, Linton Kwesi Johnson found his poetic voice in Jamaican dialect, which is retained by many black people after emigration. The special character of his poems does not just lie in the use of Jamaican vernacular, but also in the adaptation of his speaking rhythm to the beat of reggae music. His poems are fully alive only if read out loud to the beat of reggae in the form of a speech-song. Linton Kwesi Johnson has recorded most of his poems himself to the rhythms of 'dub', a musical accompaniment which accentuates beat rather than melody. In Jamaica, dub is a form of music in its own right, played, for example, by disc-jockeys who speak their own accompanying text to the dub music. Occasionally this may be very political, especially if current affairs are commented upon or if the ideas of the Rastafarians are propagated. The poems of Linton Kwesi Johnson, however, deal exclusively with the experiences of black youth in Great Britain. One of his most famous poems, *'Sonny's Lettah'* is printed below. The provocation for this poem was given by arbitrary arrests in accordance with the so-called sus law whereby any suspect person may be arrested by the police. The poem takes the form of a letter, written by young black Sonny, to his mother from Brixton Prison:

SONNY'S LETTAH
(Anti-Sus poem)

Brixton Prison,
Jebb Avenue,
London SW2,
England

Dear Mama,
Good Day.
I hope dat wen
deze few lines reach y'u,
they may find y'u in di bes' af helt.

Mama,
I really doan know how fi tell y'u dis,
cause I did mek a salim pramis
fi tek care a lickle Jim
an' try mi bes' fi look out fi him.

Mama,
Ah really did try mi bes',
but none-di-les',
mi sarry fi tell y'u seh
poor lickle Jim get arres'.

It woz di miggle a di rush howah
wen everybady jus' a hus'le an' a bus'le
fi goh home fi dem evenin' showah;
mi an' Jim stan-up
waitin' pan a bus,
nat causin' no fus',
wen all an a sudden
a police van pull-up.

Out jump t'ree policeman,
di 'bole a dem carryin' batan.
Dem waak straight up to mi an' Jim,
One a dem hol' an to Jim
seh him tekin him in;
Jim tell him fi let goh a him
far him noh dhu not'n',
an him naw t'ief,
nat even a but'n.
Jim start to wriggle.
Di police start to giggle.

Mama,
mek Ah tell y'u whey dem dhu to Jim;
Mama,
mek Ah tell y'u whey dem dhu to him:

dem t'ump him in him belly
an'it turn to jelly
dem lick him pan him back
an' him rib get pap
dem lick him pan him he'd

but it tuff like le'd
dem kick him in him seed
an' it started to bleed

Mama,
Ah jus' could'n stan-up deh
an' noh dhu not'n':
soh mi jook one in him eye
an' him started to cry;
mi t'ump one in him mout'
an' him started to shout
mi kick one pan him shin
an' him started to spin
mi t'ump him pan him chin
an' him drap pan a bin

an' crash
an de'd.

Mama,
more policeman come dung
an' beat mi to di grung;
dem charge Jim fi sus;
dem charge mi fi murdah.

Mama,
doan fret,
doan get depres'
an' doun-hearted
Be af good courage
till I hear fram you.

I remain,
your son,
Sonny.   (L.K. Johnson, 1980, pp. 7-9.)

A feeling of deep despair and powerlessness in the face
of the strength and numerical superiority of the opponent
is one message of this poem, the motto 'be af good courage'
quite another. Linton Kwesi Johnson reads his poems at
various political events and at dances. His words have an
almost electrical effect on black youth. Although at times
his constructions may be complex they are immediately

understood. His records 'Dread', 'Beat and Blood' and 'Inglan is a Bitch' have been enthusiastically received by black school pupils. They express the enormous energy of young black people, who belong to the second generation of immigrants and regard themselves as black Britons, but have to fight for their place in society against immense opposition. By contrast with the immigrant populations of Europe, their parents came to this country, because Britain bound them to herself and seduced them into identifying with British culture and way of life. Without the colonial past there would not be any Black or Asian people in the Caribbean and, equally, there would not be any black settlers in Britain.

Europe conducted a deeply contradictory policy of colonization in foreign lands, the consequences of which it is forced to bear today. Colonialism meant simultaneous attraction and repulsion, assimilation and degradation, education and stultification of the colonized. Until the wave of independence around 1960 most colonized peoples saw Britain as the sacrosanct centre of culture and civilization, a country of social justice and immense wealth. This myth was propagated by most colonial administrations of the time. It is propagated to some extent even today, in that many whites in many parts of the Third World still belong to the upper classes. Linton Kwesi Johnson talks about the first correction to his colonial view of the world when he came to England for the first time: '. . . many things were new and surprising to me. For example, seeing a white person sweeping the street- it was almost like culture shock because all the whites I knew in Jamaica, you know, drove around in big cars and smoked cigars and so on'.

The first generation of black people in Britain was brought up under 'colonial education'. The second generation, however, was born in Britain and bred in British society. The parents came as colonial subjects, their children, however, demand the same rights as their fellow white citizens. The respected Afro-Caribbean historian and cultural critic C.L.R. James, who belongs to the intellectual renaissance movement of Afro-Caribbean culture during the 1930s and 1940s, was born in Trinidad in 1901 and lives in London today. In connection with the inner-city riots of 1981 he commented on the difference between the generations as follows:

The first generation of immigrants to Britain from the Indian sub-continent, from Africa, and most notably from the West Indies, were prepared to accept some of the jobs that the white population despised. They dreamt of accumulating some money and going home to a society which they understood and where they would occupy better positions than the ones they had left behind.

The generation of blacks born or brought up here have no pattern of social development to follow. The society in which they live offers them no firm material basis nor a social perspective. Collective-ly they are not aware that they have been assigned any social significance except that which they make for themselves in their limited world. That world consists of collaboration in the streets and war with all the institutions they find themselves in–above all, with the police. Yet they are mobilised by all the stimuli of an advanced society which doesn't enable them to aim at anything or go anywhere.'   (James, 1981, p. 407.)

This new situation of direct confrontation between the narrowness of their actual situation and the manifold potential for development has evoked a contradictory response among black youngsters. On the one hand, they pursue the concept of integration in a new British society, a society which will have to be multi-ethnic and multi-cultural; on the other hand, they reject integration as a 'temptation by whites', thereby entering a phase of inner emigration. As a result of their conflict-ridden situation, numerous black adolescents adopt both attitudes, some-times alternately and sometimes simultaneously.

RASTAS AND REGGAE

The Rasta movement is perhaps the most extreme

expression of retreat to a historical African identity. Rastafarianism represents an ideology of liberation from white oppression and an attempt to find one's own identity. Religious and political thoughts are closely interwoven in this ideology. From the point of view of intellectual history, Rastafarianism further develops the pan-African ideas of Marcus Garvey. Jamaican-born, Marcus Garvey was one of the most influential exponents of black cultural renaissance before and after World War I, a renaissance which took place in the Caribbean, on the American mainland and in Africa at that time. The latter is evident in, for example, the 'Harlem-Renaissance' in the United States, 'Indigenism' in the Caribbean, 'Negritude' consciousness in the French-speaking colonies and 'Pan-Africanism' in the English-speaking colonies. The spread of these anti-colonial ideas followed the old route of the 'triangle of slavery', Africa, America and Europe, with London and Paris at the centre. The Rasta cult re-creates these old bridges in a new way. By contrast with some ideological forerunners, this cult has little to do with intellectuals, its supporters mostly live in ghettos. The Rasta cult possesses a mystical shell, the rational core of which directly refers to the century-old oppression of black people. It is hence analogous with the spirituals of the North American black slaves, which put across—in religious form—the unmistakable message about liberation from humiliation and forced labour.

The core of Rasta philosophy lies in the motto 'Back to Africa'. A whole series of Rasta ideas, however, are derived from the Christian Old Testament. This is explained by the history of missionary work during the time of slavery, when religious activity was the only cultural activity allowed to slaves. After they had been converted to Christianity, slaves were refused access to the official white Church. Therefore, being Christians, blacks began to look for a Church in accordance with their African origins. The only original, black Christian Church in Africa was the Coptic Church in Ethiopia. Ethiopia represented furthermore the only African country which had not been colonized. Hence, Ethiopia became the symbol of African identity and liberty for the Black Christians in the Caribbean. The only Christian evidence for the chosen role of Ethiopia and that of its ruler, the Lion of Judah, may be found in the Old Testament. Those passages of the Old Testament which could be interpreted as an allegory about the fate of black people, formed the actual body of ideas of the Rasta movement. When in 1930 the Ethiopian Prince Ras Tafari Makonnen was crowned the 111th Emperor of Ethiopia, this was viewed as the fulfillment of biblical prophecy, whereby the divine saviour would be resurrected as the Emperor of Ethiopia. Prince Ras Tafari named himself Emperor Haile Selassie and some groups worshipped him as God. Rastafari became a holy name and a motto for the movement. The Old Testament provided an additional identification, which gained similar importance as part of the Rasta philosophy. The blacks compared their own enslavement with the deportation of the Israelites to Babylon. The name Babylon developed as the symbol of debasement, the incarnation of all evil forces, the Israelites became synonymous with the blacks in the diaspora, as expressed by Desmond Dekker in his song 'The Israelites'. The reggae song 'By the Rivers of Babylon', interpreted by the group The Melodians, acquired world fame. This song ensured mass circulation of this kind of symbolic language:

> By the Rivers of Babylon
> Where he sat down
> And there he went
> When he remembered Zion
> But the wicked carried us away
> Captivity.
> How can we sing King Alpha's song
> In a strange land?

The text of this song leans heavily on Psalm 137. 'Babylon' and 'the wicked' designated hostile England,

London, and especially, the police. A black film of 1980, which portrays the life, ideas and imagination of black youth in London, bears the title 'Babylon'.

By means of reggae songs, the ideas of the Rasta movement spread far beyond the comparatively small group of original supporters of the cult and became known among the white population, too. However, many blacks, both in Britain and in Jamaica, vehemently disagree with the Rastas, because some of these are very sectarian and absolutely refuse any form of integration. Orthodox Rastas obey detailed instructions concerning food, clothing and way of life. Some propagate the subordination of women. Some praise the smoking of marihuana as a religious act. These atavistic tendencies led to a split in the movement, and today there is a political, progressive wing as well as an exclusively religious-mystical one.

Some of the fundamental ideas of the Rasta cult about black identity and the four hundred years of suffering in the diaspora have retained their power. The Rasta man has been elevated to a hero, a protagonist of black culture. Bob Marley embodies this archetype most completely. Although Rasta philosophy inspired him, its religious-mystical aspects lose their sectarian character in his songs, where they rather become a form of direct political and social protest. The reggae song enshrines the history of black deportation, the stigmatization of black skin, the criminalization and impoverishment in Caribbean ghettos, the depression in British 'exile'. Besides, many reggae songs are written in Jamaican dialect and therefore represent a direct expression of popular culture. Bob Marley's songs possess poetic energy, which embody the explosiveness of the real situation. The song 'Them Belly Full' is an example of this:

> Them belly full but we hungry.
> A hungry man is an angry man.
> A hungry mob is an angry mob.

Reggae music has such a comprehensive meaning for

most black youth that it engages all their energy. 'To go through the sound system', i.e. the direct experience with an electronic musical band has perhaps become the most important form of socializing for black youth. Reggae music could attain this degree of meaning and importance because it was developed solely and independently by black people. Besides, it is very young, its origins being in the late 1960s. In his poem 'Reggae Sounds', Linton Kwesi Johnson calls this type of music a 'tropical electrical storm'. Not only the sequence of words but also the characteristic rhythms expressively convey the black history of suffering: 'Dig down to the root of pain.' For Linton Kwesi Johnson, the beat of reggae represents the pulse of his people's history:

> Bass history is a moving
> is a hurting black story.
>
> (Johnson, 1975, p. 56.)

Ever since Marcus Garvey, the slogan 'Back to Africa' spreads from mouth to mouth in the black diaspora, much like the Jewish expression 'Next year in Jerusalem'. However, 'Back to Africa' is not understood in the literal sense by most black Britons, but as a direct appeal to mentally reflect upon their African origins. The song 'Africa' by the group 'Mighty Diamonds' provides a good example:

> Africa is the land of home, yeah,
> Africa is the land where I and I come from,
> Africa our father's land is calling us home,
> So long we've been slaves and no more will we roam.
>
> So I will hope and pray that the day will come
> When we will see the rising sun.
> When no more crying, no victimising,
> No more starvation, no more
> No more killing.

Some black prople in the diaspora, however, did attempt

to emigrate back to Africa. Liberia and Sierra Leone are foundations of former slaves. In Ethiopia, there are small enclaves of supporters of the Rasta movement from the years of its beginning before World War II. Numerous additional blacks decided during the course of the 1960s, to devote their labour, knowledge and skills to the newly emerging, independent African societies. Frantz Fanon of Martinique went to Algeria as a medical doctor and George Padmore of Trinidad came to Ghana as an adviser to Kwame Nkrumah. However, they are exceptions and for the overwhelming majority of blacks in the diaspora, there just is no question of emigration. Four hundred years of slavery and colonialism represent reality, a reality which has shaped their past history as well as present identity and which cannot therefore be undone by re-emigrating to Africa.

EMIGRATION: LIBERATION AND ILLUSION

Black immigration during the twentieth century has made Britain a multi-ethnic country. The country's imperial past lives on in the form of ethnic minorities. It appears to be an irony of history that after the dissolution of her Empire Britain will have to deal with the human consequences of colonization within her own boundaries. The colonial past has caught up with Great Britain.

During both world wars thousands of black soldiers served in the British Army. Woodcutters from British Honduras came to Scotland, machine operators from Jamaica worked in British ammunition factories and black women served as nurses in military hospitals. Afterwards many of them found permanent employment and stayed. During the 1950s, both full employment and an expanding British economy were the main reasons for the launching of recruitment campaigns. London Transport, in particular, signed contracts in the colonies themselves with local people seeking jobs. The arrival of ships transporting emigrants from the Caribbean at the port of Southampton became a familiar symbol of the new wave of immigrants. The 1948 Nationality Act extended British citizenship to all citizens of the colonies and the Commonwealth, although people did not then receive a British passport. The Nationality Act formed the legal basis for unrestricted movement, which took place in both directions. When, at the beginning of the 1960s, the number of people from Africa, Asia and the Caribbean in the UK amounted to about half a million people, the first restrictive controls were implemented. Initially it was hoped to contain immigration by issuing only a limited number of work permits annually. These measures were gradually but progressively tightened up. In 1981, Margaret Thatcher's Conservative Government passed a new Nationality Act.

From then on, all holders of British Nationality overseas do not automatically possess the right of abode within the United Kingdom. This measure is aimed at refusing the numerous coloured British passport holders entry into the UK (like, for instance, the Indians in Africa or the Chinese in Hong Kong). The case of the expulsion of Indians from Uganda, who were British passport holders, has shown that certain situations may suddenly arise, where Great Britain will be reminded of her colonial obligations from which she would gladly be released. The new nationality regulations carry the risk of making thousands of coloured Britons *de facto* stateless. This is because some categories of British overseas passports do not carry the right of entry into other countries either. All these measures also mean that Western passports will be yet more privileged regarding unrestricted travel. Hence they could become valuable objects of speculation for *declassé* citizens of the Third World. Colonialism as a whole has created problems both by causing massive migration of people in a wide variety of different ways and by the destruction of developed social structures in the colonies themselves. These problems were not solved by formal declarations of independence, instead they were made visible.

Emigration has remained the most fundamental experience in the lives of black Britons. They have become eternal emigrants and strangers. They are 'in transit' all the time, as it says in a contemporary black play. In a collection of interviews with black Britons, the American social psychologist Thomas J. Cottle recorded what one of the interviewees, Sonny Peterson, said: 'You give us a great deal when you emigrate. . . We've come here, thousands like us, we've come here, but we haven't arrived. You get my meaning? We haven't arrived. We're here, but that's all we are. We had to fight that battle; we're still fighting it, just being here.' (Cottle, 1978, p. 18.)

The search for employment was just one reason for emigrating. The motivation for emigration also springs from the powerful desire to determine the course of one's life for the first (and perhaps only) time. Sonny Peterson continues: '. . . immigrating was the only step of freedom many of us could take, no matter how good or bad it came out'. (Cottle, 1978, p. 22.)

Emigration as the fate of a whole generation is the leading motif in many novels by West Indian authors. For instance, George Lamming's novel *The Emigrants* (1954) vividly portrays personal tragedy and human disintegration of a group of West Indians who, after their arrival in England, are condemned to a life of perpetual wandering and search, from flat to flat, work to work, looking for people who disperse in the crowd and looking for ways to earn their living. In Lamming's novel, West Indian immigrants live in the nooks and crannies of British society, utterly demoralized. One of the leading figures is Dickson of Barbados, a teacher, who has always understood himself as being a 'black Englishman'. In England, however, this conception of himself, which has shaped his previous life, is taken away. A human wreck remains. Below, the author describes the deep-seated illusion, which has seduced black West Indians of his generation into a false identity:

I had no great liking for Dickson, but I suddenly felt that Dickson's fate might in a way have been awaiting me, or any man who chose one country rather than another in the illusion that it was only a larger extension of the home which he had left. For it would be a lie to deny that on the ship and even in the hostel, there was a feeling, more conscious in some than others, that England was not only a place, but a heritage. Some of us might have expressed a certain hostility to that heritage, but it remained, nevertheless, a hostility to something that was already a part of us.

But all that was now coming to an end. England was simply a world which we had moved about at random, and on occasions encountered by chance. It was just there like nature, drifting vaguely beyond our reach.   (Lamming, 1980, pp. 228–9.)

The illusion of being a black Englishman is related to the illusion of somehow, sometime acquiring riches in England. Samuel Selvon, who was born in Trinidad and came to England in 1950, wrote the novel *The Lonely Londoners*, published in 1956. The novel deals with a group of West Indians living in the Bayswater area of London who dream the dream of the high life while living in basement flats. For example, 'Big City', a black man who had grown up in an orphanage in Trinidad, was given this nickname by his friends because he was always talking of the great cities of the world: ' "Big city for me," he would say. "None of this smalltime village life for me. Is New York and London and Paris, that is big life. You think I going to stay in Trinidad when the war over? This small place?" ' (Selvon, 1979, p. 78.)

'Big City' became a sailor, travelled all over and one day in London he purposely missed his ship, because he wanted to get to know the high life. Now he was living in this huge city, ignoring his miserable existence by dreaming every day a different dream of the high life. He was living in an imaginary London, which had as little to do with reality as the street names he kept making up or distorting. He hardly knew the proper names of this big new world, let alone what lies behind them, but his self-deception acquired more reality for him than the real world. Here he boasted about getting to know a rich lady: 'I was coasting a time by the Circus, and a big limousine pull up, and the driver ask me if I from the West Indies, and I say yes, and then he say that Lady—want to meet a West Indian, if I would come. So you should know I hop in the car—car, father, boy—and we drive to Millionaires Road.' (Selvon, 1979, p. 85.)

An exaggerated dream of integration dominated the imagination of many immigrants of the first generation. The newcomer imagines the new society to be the opposite to the one he or she has just left; a society without poverty, without class differences and without racial barriers. This first generation sees itself in the 1980s, branded by the next generation as remnants of the colonial era, as 'Uncle Toms'. Andrew Salkey's novel *Danny Jones* portrays four black teenagers in Ladbroke Grove (North London) who think of England as 'Deception Isles'. All opportunities appear barred to them, by the school, the police and their own parents. The father of Danny Jones, who comes from Jamaica, feels rejected by his own son:

My son sees me as a man who stopped growing and developing as a person, years and years ago, in Jamaica. He's pigeon-holed me as this incredible colonial of his, some sort of obedient servant of a long-dead Queen Victoria and Victorian England, some sort of black man so in love with England and white values and achievements that he's no longer a black man but a white black man. An Uncle Tom.   (Salkey, 1980, p. 68.)

Towards the end of the novel, both Danny Jones and his parents return to Jamaica. Is repatriation a solution?

According to the director of the independent Institute of Race Relations, A. Sivanandan, who is also editor of the journal *Race & Class*, public debate on Britain's black population is not only characterized by hostility but also causes many black people to adopt defensive attitudes which in turn makes many of them leave the country. A. Sivanandan calls this public campaign 'induced repatriation'. The majority of blacks, however, feel British and wish to remain so. Britain in the past regarded herself as a purely white society, although at the same time she saw herself as an Empire composed of a diversity of peoples living in a wide variety of lands. Britain has now been caught up by her own history and refuses to accept at home what it has propagated abroad. Colonial ideology gave rise to a peculiar contradiction, as a matter of course the British nation would be ethnically, culturally and politically homogenous, but the colonial territories were postulated as naturally heterogenous. Britain still possesses a false self-conception, because the break with her colonial past has not been a conscious or collective process. Neither have the Scottish, Welsh and Irish peoples been granted adequate independence to this day: devolution for Scotland and Wales did not happen, and Ireland remains partitioned. Nor have black people with their different cultural and ethnic origins been accepted. The new Great Britain will have to stay true to what it always wanted to be as a colonial Empire: a multiracial state.

One of the most disastrous effects of racial or class oppression consists in the fact that despotism on the part of the government will be answered in the form of destructive action on the part of the governed. The power of the forces ensuring 'law and order' generates a feeling of chaotic and complete helplessness in the oppressed, which in turn can set free desolate, self-destructive energies. 'Tribal war in a Babylon' reads a line in a reggae song. Pent-up aggression of black youth quite often explodes in fighting among themselves. The permanent threat posed by the social environment leads to demoralization, exhaustion and destruction. Linton Kwesi Johnson deals with these problems in several poems and names the consequences:

> Rebellion rushing doun the wrong road,
> Storm blowing doun the wrong tree. . .
>
> (Johnson, 1975, p. 17.)

In his poem *Doun de road*, Johnson furthermore

directly relates the self-destructive fights among the blacks themselves to the racist forces operating in the society at large:

DOUN DE ROAD

heavy heavy terror
on the rampage. . .
o dont you worry
it is so near. . .
fatricide is only
the first phase. . .

yes, the violence of the oppressor runnin wild;
them pickin up the yout them fe suss;
powell prophesying a black, a black, a black conquest;
and the National Front is on the rampage
making fire bombs fe burn we.

terror fire terror fire reach we:
such a suffering we suffering
in this burning age of rage;
no place to run to get gun
and the violence damming up inside.

so in the heat
of the anguish
you jus turn:
turn on your brother
an yu lick him

an yu lash him
an stab him
an kill him

and the violence damming up inside.

O that history should take such a rough route,
causing us this bitterness and pain on the way,
is a room full of a fact you cant walk out;

fatricide is only the first phase,
with brother fighting brother stabbing brother;
them jus killing off them one another,

but when you see your brother blood jus flow:
futile fighting; then you know
that the first phase must come to an end
and time for the second phase to show.

Mistrust and embitterment prevail in all coloured groups, whether they be of Afro-Caribbean or Asian origin. The tendency to escape into mental and physical ghettos threatens to wreck every achievement. It seems as if, in the existing society, differences among people, which can be very fruitful and enriching, sometimes change completely into mutually exclusive, hostile and violent contrasts.

The chaos of the first phase must come to a close. What, however, will the second phase look like? As Civil Rights leader Dr Martin Luther King, Jr., put it in the title of his last major analytical book, published while he was still alive: *Where Do We Go From Here: Chaos or Community?*

CHAPTER FIVE

The intellectual
and the
transformation of society

PHILOSOPHY OF PERMANENT CRISIS

The spectre of revolution has appeared only once in Britain in this century. It disappeared as rapidly as it rose, resulting in a demoralized working class and a victorious bourgeoisie which at first could hardly believe its victory and later took advantage of it ruthlessly. This brief moment of deep domestic upheaval was the General Strike of 1926. Since World War I, all of Europe had been in a state of ferment, and in the aftermath of the Russian Revolution the British ruling classes feared revolution much more than could be justified by any actual planning of, let alone active preparation for, revolution from below. The subsequent collapse of the 'British revolution' was taken by its opponents as confirmation of their self-righteous and intolerant belief in the superiority of the prevailing system. The predominant intelligentsia legitimized a renewed national consensus, allegedly neutral of class, between a humiliated working class and a blindly self-confident bourgeoisie.

Under the impression of the failed General Strike, the novelist John Galsworthy developed a picture of English society and English national character which remains characteristic of English self-assessment even today. He describes a society with permanent proneness to crisis, without actual crisis. In his preface to *A Modern Comedy* he compares the situation of society in the late 1920s with the situation in the late 1880s, the beginning of the *Forsyte Saga.* To begin with, he states a loss of purposefulness. Modern times had lost a conception of the future. The English nation have adapted to inadequacies and learnt to live with scarcities, and even draw from this a new advantage:

We are still a people that cannot be rushed, distrustful of extremes, saved by the grace of our defensive humour, well tempered, resentful of interference, improvident and wasteful, but endowed with a certain genius for recovery. If we believe in nothing much else, we still believe in ourselves. That salient characteristic of the English will bear thinking about. Why, for instance, do we continually run ourselves down? Simply because we have not got the inferiority complex and are indifferent to what other people think of us. No people in the world seems openly less sure of itself; no people is secretly more sure.   (Galsworthy, 1958, p. xiii.)

This combination of outward hesitation and insecurity and inner unshakeable self-confidence persists today. It dominates present-day discussion on the situation of the nation. Since the late 1970s, crisis, decline, decay of the old order, dissolution of an obsolete system of values are central issues of public debate, academic theses, journalistic articles and even literature. Public opinion is certain that Britain is undergoing deep and decisive transformation. However, public discussion of the country's crisis is conducted with a degree of self-assuredness which resembles the Galsworthy analysis and which commands respect and acclaim by the foreign observer. Despite a massive wave of strikes in the 1970s, despite riots in the inner cities and the closure of factories, despite the virtual de-industrialization of entire areas (such as Merseyside), despite mass unemployment and impoverishment, the British nation still displays a degree of stability and homogeneity which appears to contradict what is commonly meant by the concept of 'crisis'.

What kind of transformation is British society under-going? Is it really a fundamental transformation involving structural changes in society or is the current debate on crisis merely a reflection of this periodic complaint of every generation 'that things are not what they used to be'?

There are obvious indications among the British intelligentsia that the growing awareness of crisis is *real.* For example, in her latest four-volume novel *Canopus in Argos*, writer Doris Lessing conjures up a picture of extinction and destruction not just of Britain, but the world at large. Apocalyptic Hollywood films are significant for Britain, too. *Towering Inferno, Earthquake, Airport* belong to the most popular pictures. Academics and journalists of every complexion analyze the crisis. They may come to different conclusions regarding the nature of the crisis, but they all agree on its existence. This tendency is demonstrated by a recent series of publications bearing dramatic titles like *Is Britain dying?*, *Britain in Decline*, *The Wasting of the British Economy.*

The same premises are evident in the work of commentators like Karl-Heinz Bohrer in his collection of essays *Ein bißchen Lust am Untergang* (1979) and Professor Samuel H. Beer from Harvard University in his latest book *Britain against itself: The Political Contradictions of Collectivism* (1982). Professor Beer has been expert on Britain for decades and his 1965 book *Modern British Politics* is now a classic: there Great Britain was depicted as the prime example of civic culture, a shining model of stable democracy. Today, Samuel Beer takes Britain as a model for the failure of democracy. He argues that one of the most essential preconditions for the functioning of any society is the certainty of its citizens that the basic rules of society will be adhered to by everyone. This basic trust shapes the basis of social consensus, and it is precisely this trust which Britain has lost. The result has been fragmentation of power, or, as Beer puts it, a 'self-destructive Hobbesian struggle of pluralistic stagnation'. This particular analysis was developed from a liberal viewpoint. It re-emerged with the new Social Democratic Party's call upon 'a new consensus under new trust'. One of the leading lights of the SDP, party president Mrs Shirley Williams, was lecturing at Harvard at about the same time as Professor Beer was writing his new book. Samuel Beer's hopes for the future of British society rest with the 'renewal of their radical tradition'. 'Radical' here probably means 'liberal' in the sense of nineteenth century liberalism. According to the liberal middle classes, the crisis of British society consists of a general and considerable decline in confidence in archaic structures and obsolete organizations, including the Conservative and Labour parties. Hence the foundation of the SDP as a new party of new trust. Shirley Williams's own research and reflections on Britain's political and economic future have been published in her recent books *Politics is for People* (1981) and *A Job to Live* (1985). Right-wing thinking is diametrically opposed to this analysis. Not too few, but too many changes accelerated Britain's decline over the past thirty years. Therefore, right-wing hopes aim for radical restoration rather than radical reform. This New Right argues that the development of a new power structure in Britain is the cause of the crisis. This view is exemplified by journalist Paul Johnson who writes in his recent review of Samuel Beer's analysis and of the revised, classic portrait of England by Anthony Sampson (*The Changing Anatomy of Britain*, 1982):

If one is asked where power in Britain lies today one might be inclined to answer: everywhere—and nowhere. Power has become very widely diffused in Britain, but it is chiefly negative power: the right or ability to prevent, impede, destroy, delay and brake. The problem is how to create a superior concentration of positive and creative power, which can carry us into the twenty-first century in reasonably good shape. It is not clear how this can be done, but I suspect that in the end it may well be by a return to traditional English values and by a wholesale repudiation of the 1960s' conventional wisdom.

(Johnson, 1982, *Times Literary Supplement.*)

The crisis of society is interpreted as a shift of powers traditionally assigned to the state. Less government and more government is demanded in one breath. Less government in the ideological battle against 'collectivism' and 'socialism', to use the language of right-wing thinking. This has not changed since the nineteenth century when Herbert Spencer introduced the still current dichotomy of liberalism, 'Individual Freedom versus State-coercion', as part of the crusade against the 'slavery of socialism'; long before workers possessed real power of any sort. More government is demanded for the purposes of law and order and for the prohibition of alternative structures of power, be they provided by unions, cooperatives or regional self-government. Spencer formulated his ideas on 'Man versus State' at a time when the British Empire had reached its maximum expansion, representing one of the crudest exercises of state power. Today, when conservative philosophers demand less government, they do not apply this demand to the state *per se* or as a whole, but only to certain aspects of its development: in particular those areas run by the state which represent the economic back-up for the poor and needy, such as the National Health Service, public works and public job-creation programmes, state education and nationalized industries. On the other hand and at the same time, the strengthening of public authorities designed to maintain law and order is demanded; the police forces, the armed forces and the judiciary. The battle of ideas against the background of contemporary crisis of British society represents more than ever a battle between classic conservative positions and socialist-type philosophies. Remarkably, the Right bluntly names this confrontation for what it is; the Left is much less clear and coherent regarding the articulation of its ideas. This disadvantage is not primarily due to lack of programmes or objectives, but to a deficit in the tradition of theoretical thinking in Britain.

THE BRITISH WAY OF DOING THINGS

The evaluation and reputation of theory is another important element in British self-assessment. There is a widespread feeling for 'the British way of doing things' applicable to problems in scientific, political, industrial or everyday life. People will only hesitantly commit themselves to define vaguely this 'British method'. This method was a result of the specific social and industrial history of the country. The principle of expediency is all-important. The elaboration of theoretical models when problem solving is explicitly considered 'un-British'.

For example, in the preface of E.W. Heley's recent book (1981) on educational reform, the following sentence attempted to explain the existence of a multitude of experimental school types in Great Britain: 'It is the habit of the English. . . to distrust a philosophical approach to problems.' Also, during EEC negotiations, former Foreign Secretary Lord Carrington was asked to define the British position regarding the Community. He rejected any form of definition by remarking that continental people were constantly enquiring about theories and programmes in connection with the EEC, whereas British people prefered pragmatic solutions to particular problems. Furthermore, in a contemporary textbook designed for foreigners (*Life in Britain*), P. Bromhead writes at the beginning 'The English tend to avoid precise definitions.' This self-understanding does not only touch on the principle of proceeding pragmatically, but also above all all on the rejection of theory as unhelpful and confusing and, in thinking about society, even detrimental.

One of the most important British conservative thinkers, Edmund Burke, condemned the French Revolution, of which he was a contemporary, not primarily because of the tremendous loss of life it caused but because of the explicit attempt to translate abstract principles into social praxis. This would mean a fatal intervention in history by man. Half a century later, even cosmopolitan thinker

Matthew Arnold rejects Jacobinism in his book *Culture and Anarchy* primarily because of its endeavour to transform society in the light of a doctrine by 'elaborating down to the very smallest details a rational society for the future'. This 'anti-doctrinaire' viewpoint was elevated by Benjamin Disraeli to a national political 'doctrine'. Since then, this attitude has become more and more firmly established as part of the principal credo of conservative thinking. Disraeli wrote in 1868:

In a progressive country, change is constant, and the great question is not whether you should resist change which is inevitable, but whether that change should be carried out in deference to the manners, customs, laws and traditions of a people, or whether it should be carried out in deference to abstract principle and arbitrary and general doctrines. The one is a national system, the other. . . a philosophical system.

(*The Times* 15 February 1980, quoted in an article by K. Middlemas.)

When public discussion associated Margaret Thatcher with the theory of monetarism and its leading exponents like F.A. Hajek and Milton Friedman, she explicitly depicted her economic strategy as a return to old values rather than the result of a new theory. In 1980, she explained in an address to journalists: 'We do not want to support the takeover of dogmas and formulae. We support the restoration of those old and proven values, which in the past have made this nation great.'

It would be mistaken to interpret this rejection of theory in British thinking as an outright hostility to theoretical thinking. For only a particular comprehension of theory is actually rejected. In Britain, theory is not understood as being the rational and necessary precondition for practical achievements. The deep and widespread appreciation of practical knowledge is the result of historical experience. It was able to develop into an integral part of national ideology because the industrial revolution led to the sharing of this experience by large sections of the population. It was not the qualified scientists or knowledgeable engineers who pioneered the industrial revolution, but the master artisans and craftsmen who designed by daily experimentation—and without theoretical education—the fundamental machines of industrialization. These machines were perfected and theoretically re-created by others only later. The development of spinning and weaving machines exemplifies how practical people came to design machines which were eventually capable of combing, cleansing, de-greasing, spinning and weaving. Much practical knowledge about the daily difficulties of dealing with the raw material, wool, clearly enabled them to do so. Even today British workers and engineers take a different attitude to dealing with machines to that of, for instance, their German counterparts. Foreign observers of British factories may still be astounded by the amazing extent to which un-written knowledge and long accumulated experience is handed down from one generation to the next. As much of this experience is stored in the hearts and minds of people, it is in danger of being lost forever by continuing de-industrialization.

To summarize we could say that the British way of doing things incorporates not only the belief that practical developments do not usually require theoretical foundations, but furthermore that praxis is at its best if kept free of theoretical interference. This does not mean that scientific research of particular problems is neglected, quite the contrary; but it does mean that the ideological comprehension of theory is different in Britain to what it is, for example, in Germany.

CONSERVATIVE THINKING AND NATIONAL HERITAGE

Because of the historical juxtaposition and the political estimation of theory and praxis, the British philosophical tradition has come to associate the concept of 'pragmatism' with conservative thinking and the outline of social theories with socialist thinking. Therefore, the battle between conservative and socialist philosophies displays an unique ideological asymmetry in Britain. Since socialism and social progress assume at first a theoretical character, they are felt to counter the traditional British way of doing things. Hence conservative thinking is deeply rooted in national thinking. The following maxim is still very important to conservative politicians: the less we theorize, the more time is going to work for us. Many conservative slogans are so profoundly intertwined with the country's history and traditions that even critical intellectuals find them inextricably bound up in the national heritage.

Even today, the myth holds sway of Britain's history being essentially the history of its Parliament and its development. Parliament represents a national shrine, the class political derivation of which still has no chance at all to penetrate public perception. Therefore, many Conservative aims, serving purely party political interest, are nevertheless widely propagated, because they are generally perceived as belonging to the national philosophical heritage. The slogan *'religion, liberty and property, the old parliamentarian trinity'* represents a good example of this. Britain's recent history has seen no revolution. Consequently, the country has never broken with the past and its institutions. Hence, even among left-wing intellectuals a unique sense of identity with British custom and traditions has developed. They are laboriously attempting to elaborate a left-wing national tradition of their own, which they hope to see incorporated into British national thinking. Long ago, the labour movement had shown the way, and its own history is well documented. This history may be said to begin with the Peasants' Revolt of 1381, continuing with the seventeenth century's English Revolution by the levellers and diggers, the massacre of Peterloo, the Tolpuddle martyrs, the Chartist movement, and the first Unions and Labour Members of Parliament up to the battles of our time. Some left-wing intellectuals have conducted research into historical aspects of the labour movement and wrote classical treatises such as *The Making of the English Working Class* by E.P. Thompson and Eric Hobsbawm's *Industry and Empire*. Today, innumerable collections of so-called oral history are made to illustrate the as-yet-unwritten history of common people. But where is the analysis of that part of the national heritage consisting of the social and philosophical thinking which adopts the point of view of the lower classes? Will this field continue to be a stronghold of conservative academics and writers? Britain did not produce someone like Antonio Gramsci in Italy or Rosa Luxemburg in Germany, not least because the country was spared the traumatic upheavals and devastation of war and fascism. The seething unrest of the 1930s, however, led for the first time to the formation of a socialist intelligentsia founded on a broad basis. World War II destroyed these first signs of a firm tradition. Christopher Caudwell, for example, was killed in the Spanish Civil War, before he was able to deepen and develop his social and cultural criticism of British society into a fundamental and lasting analysis of the nation. Only individuals such as Marxist writer and literary critic Raymond Williams actually continued from these beginnings once World War II was over. His example furthermore shows how difficult it was for his generation who had practically to start 'from scratch'. Raymond Williams' *Culture and Society 1780-1950*, published in 1958, represented one of the first analyses of social revolutionary thinking in Britain in its relation to national tradition. In this book, he deals with both radical and conservative thinkers. For instance, he analyses the work of William Cobbet who formulated the 'practical' conclusion that the labour of the poor represents the source of wealth for the rich long before Karl Marx set down his 'theoretical' reasoning for the same conclusion. But Raymond Williams also looked into the emancipatory tendencies and social criticism of conservative writers such as Edmund Burke.

On the whole, however, such attempts to re-write the

history of British thinking remain individual instances only. An overall coherent conceptual model, which would not only be critical of society, but would attempt to interpret national culture from the perspective of the working classes, is lacking to this day. If existent, such a model could possibly be widely adopted as well as serving as a guideline for action. There are some general models concerning the British transition to socialism, either written by individual intellectuals or small political parties, e.g. the programme of the Communist Party, *The British Road to Socialism*. These attempts, however, represent hardly more than 'dead paper', because they are not widely adopted.

From a continental perspective, the British left-wing intellectual displays deep loyalty towards the British nation and state. He identifies himself with the national heritage of his own country to a much larger and unbroken extent than his German counterpart would. When nowadays public debate focusses on the question of what degree of consensus the British people have retained or lost, then the very existence of the debate implies the fact that national homogeneity constituted an important part of recent national history. This homogeneity of national cultural heritage has had two negative consequences: firstly, cultural history has been written primarily and most effectively from a conservative perspective; secondly, many intellectual rebels did not voice their opposition in terms of class, but in terms of *national* grievances. British thinking contains a characteristic mixture of conservative loyalty to Queen and country as well as a progressive perspective which detects deplorable states of affairs or abuses of power. This mixture could hardly be found anywhere else; and even early writers like Jonathan Swift, Edmund Burke and Thomas Babington Macaulay clearly reveal it. Outside academia, this dichotomy of British thinking particularly applies to that most important type of modern intellectual who is not only loyally devoted to the state, but who virtually mass-fabricates official consensus: the journalist. In the British society of today, famous journalists have assumed an almost grotesque degree of importance. Well-known newsreaders open kindergartens and popular commentators are knighted by the Queen. The actual integration of the intellectual into the state machinery is certainly not any deeper than in most European countries. However, his intense sense of identity with conservative patterns of national reflection makes this integration appear stronger than it really is. One of the most important reasons for this feeling of identity was the combined absence of fascism and revolution in Britain. No fascist ruler banned, extradited or murdered thousands of intellectuals and no revolution demanded that the intellectuals produce clear evidence of partiality. Probably unlike any other great European nation, the position of the intellectual in British society has never been hotly contested or seriously challenged. Since the state never became in reality the enemy of the intellectuals, it was never really perceived as such.

Only the social changes of the late 1960s, the expansion of the university sector in particular, enabled intellectuals both to rise from the lower strata of society and to continue the interrupted tradition of the 1930s. These changes have begun to produce a new kind of left-wing intellectual who understands the concept of being left-wing not only as a general position of social criticism, but additionally views it as a declaration of support for the concerns and objectives of the labour movement. This new type of left-wing intellectual increases in importance, although hesitantly so, because the problems of the working class have become centrally relevant to the nation. This alone, however, is not going to break the overriding dominance of conservative views in British thinking.

For the Britain of today, its own past greatness has become a terrible obstacle. The shadow of the Empire weighs heavily on Britain's outlook today. The native tongue of the British people has undoubtedly become the undisputed world language. Thereby, every British native inherits a kind of universalism which confers a natural advantage to the nation in many areas. If this universalism, in the colonial tradition, manifests itself as self-sufficiency of the Anglo-Saxon world, then it may be more aptly described as cosmopolitan provincialism. 'Universal provincialism' is reminiscent of Galsworthy's formula, whereby the more self-confidence British people have, the more insecure they appear. Particularly in the area of politics, this self-confidence is not so much trust in one's own strength, but, much more frequently, blind adherence to familiar attitudes, approaches and institutions.

E.P. THOMPSON: MORRISISM AND THE BRITISH WAY TO SOCIALISM

The strong sense of identity with national tradition and its institutions among intellectuals led to considerable confidence, among the advocats of a socialist transformation of British society, in the possibility of developing an independent British way to socialism, and that since at least about 1880, when Karl Marx began to be more widely influential. Tony Benn, one of the leading left-wing Labour politicians, and the one among them who has formulated perhaps one of the clearest and most radical strategies for structural social change states expressly that he is not a Marxist. Instead of Karl Marx, he quotes a wide variety of political currents representing British emancipatory movements: the non-conformist churches, the levellers and diggers, the Chartist movement and the tradition of British socialists.

Even if a politician like Tony Benn emphasizes national independence in socialist thinking, perhaps for political reasons, it must be added that a large proportion of left-wing intellectuals would agree with him. Historian E. P. Thompson may be taken as representative of left-wing thinkers. Today, he is one of the leading personalities of the peace movement and has let his academic work take second place to his participation in the coordinating committee of the European Movement for Nuclear Disarmament (END). Today his charismatic personality plays a similar role in the British peace movement to Bertrand Russell's in the late 1950s. When the government issued the brochure *Protect and Survive* to aid civil defence, Thompson wrote a satirical rejoinder entitled *Protest and Survive* which developed into a kind of manifesto of the whole movement. In 1981, E.P. Thompson was supposed to give the annual Richard Dimbleby Lecture of the BBC and thereby outline the views of supporters of unilateral nuclear disarmament. His invitation was withdrawn on pressure by the director general of the BBC, Ian Trethowan.

E.P. Thompson has become an intellectual of national stature. His interventions have become a political matter, because the debate on peace and disarmament is closely tied up with the question of Britain's future role in world affairs: should the country remain a leading nuclear power and thereby perpetuate its old imperial position at a different level?

E.P. Thompson originates from an intellectual family. His father was a writer, missionary and professor at Oxford. Thompson himself was educated at Cambridge and held lectureships at the Universities of Leeds and Warwick. His first important academic work dealt with William Morris, who, during the second half of his life, travelled as a professional agitator from political meeting to political meeting in order to propagate Marxism. Morris' personal diaries during those years represent one of the most important historical documents on the political awareness of the British labour movement around 1880. E.P. Thompson was thirty-one years old when his book on Morris was published in 1955. He says that this work deeply influenced his opinions concerning an independent British traditional line to socialism. There is a parallel with Raymond Williams' *Culture and Society*. Both authors attempted independently to tackle the task of historically retracing the tradition of socialist thinking. The romantic criticism of utilitarianism and the utopian critique of capitalism were their investigative end-points. Thompson's book on Morris was virtually ignored by the academic world. A review in the *Times Literary Supplement* misunderstood it as merely long-winded polemics putting the Communist case against Morris.

One year after the publication of the Morris book, the events in Hungary led Thompson to come into fundamental conflict with the Communist Party. He resigned his membership and subsequently became a member of the Labour Party. In his epilogue to a new edition of *William Morris* Thompson writes in 1977 to clarify his position: 'The Morris/Marx argument has worked inside me ever since. When, in 1956, my disagreements with orthodox Marxism became fully articulate, I fell back on modes of perception which I'd learned in those years of close company with Morris. . .' (Thompson, 1977, p. 810.)

E.P. Thompson still calls himself a Marxist, distancing himself from non-informed attacks against Marx. But with regard to any systematic exegesis of Marx, he would call himself a supporter of Morris: 'I'm a Morrisist, which has an affinity and a dialogue with Marx himself but which also has a Utopian element in it.' (Thompson, *The Times*, 3 August 1981.)

This utopian element is related in particular to the moral dimension of social struggles as well as to the conscious effort to imagine the utopia of liberated mankind. In an open letter to Leszek Kolakowski, written in 1973, Thompson outlines such an utopian dream:

My own utopia, two hundred years ahead, would not be like Morris's 'epoch of rest'. It would be a world (as D.H. Lawrence would have it) where the 'money values' give way before the 'life values', or (as Blake would have it) 'corporeal' will give way to 'mental' war. With sources of power easily available, some men and women might choose to live in unified communities, sited, like Cistercian monasteries, in centres of great natural beauty, where agricultural, industrial and intellectual pursuits might be combined. Others might prefer the variety and pace of an urban life which rediscovers some of the qualities of the city-state. Others will prefer a life of seclusion, and many will pass between all three. Scholars would follow the disputes of different schools, in Paris, Jakarta or Bogata.

(Thompson, 1974, p. 78.)

E.P. Thompson continued to be an active intellectual after he left the Communist Party. He promoted the formation of a New Left, in connection with the political magazine *New Left Review*. This New Left remained an independent grouping. It acted to further the reception of Marx in Great Britain, although without the support of Thompson, and is partly of Trotskyist orientation. In 1960, Thompson and some of his colleagues issued the pamphlet *Out of Apathy* which outlines a revolutionary model for Britain. Thompson clearly marked the limits to so-called 'catastrophe models of revolution', as he referred to the historic examples of 1789 France and 1917 Tsarist Russia:

It is possible to look forward to a peaceful revolution in Britain, with far greater continuity in social life and in institutional forms than would have seemed likely even twenty years ago, not because it will be a semi-revolution, nor because capitalism is 'evolving' into socialism; but because the advances of 1942–48 *were* real, because the socialist *potential* has been enlarged, and socialist forms, however imperfect, have grown up 'within' capitalism.

(Thompson, 1960, p. 302.)

E.P. Thompson argues that the most favourable moment for revolution would lie in what he termed an 'historic watershed'. This watershed situation together with increased political activity of the entire people—for or against revolution—would lead to a sudden and complete change in the conditions of the old power structure on all levels of society. In this context, some of the key institutions of the old order would have to be abolished—like the House of Lords, the Stock Exchange and the press monopoly. Other key institutions would have to be adapted to the requirements of the new order—like the House of Commons, the administration of the nationalized industries or worker representation through shop stewards. The answer to the question how exactly to envisage this break with the prevailing system is quite revealing as far as the theory of a British way to socialism is concerned. With astounding straightforwardness, E.P. Thompson refers back to the 'British way of doing things', not merely because it is British, but because it represents a kind of 'national approach' which people have internalized: 'What it is more important to insist upon is that it is necessary to *find out* the breaking point, not by theoretical speculation alone, but *in practice* by unrelenting reforming pressures in many fields, which are designed to reach a revolutionary culmination.' (Thompson, 1960, p. 303.)

Here again praxis is stressed as proving or providing evidence for truth, because only in praxis can theory be fully unfolded. Hence, the main task of politically active people lies in both the grasping of historic moments (which develop as a result of praxis) and acting adequately as a result. Consequently, Thompson sharply criticized the construction of theoretical models by French marxist Louis Althusser in 1980, for instance. He designates this the 'poverty of theory': too many models with too little relation to reality.

The important question is why this 'break' with the old order has not yet happened. Is a fundamental shift in the familiar structure of power developing in the 1980s? Thompson's analysis of Britain's present historical phase is of particular interest. He considers the Britain of 1960 not just 'ripe' but 'overripe' for socialism. In other words, the most appropriate moment of a historic turn-about has already passed. Thompson sees a danger here for the overall development of society in that. Does this mean that Britain's present crisis must be understood primarily as a crisis of the labour movement which has missed its historic opportunity and task? In 1980, Eric Hobsbawm, in *Forward March of Labour Halted*, also focused upon a historic standstill of the British labour movement, albeit from a different political perspective. Assessing British society of today is particularly difficult, as the political tendencies of restoration and radicalization not only move in opposite directions, but appear equally strong. It is probably only in retrospect that we will be able to see which phenomenon will have achieved historic dominance.

One of the most striking characteristics of contemporary cultural life in Britain is the political commitment of many inellectuals *outside* party political or professional organizations. The peace movement represents the biggest and most influential form of this commitment at present. E.P. Thompson's example is quite typical. Social groupings of this sort do not substitute for political parties, although some participants might subjectively feel this to be the case. They represent a qualitatively new organizational expression of democracy. They have considerable attraction for intellectuals who are not active at the party political level and create possibilities for incorporating them into social struggles. These possibilities may range from tenants' associations and campaigns for council housing; to pressure groups dealing with problems of road construction, public transport or the environment generally; to associations looking into the powers and practices of the police and the judiciary; to organizations of the coloured population as well as the women's movement. The latter is one of the socially most significant associations, despite its organizational fragmentation. Furthermore, there are a series of communal institutions, which embody a significant degree of local government and local autonomy, like the Health Councils and Law Centres.

All these social groupings represent qualitatively new kinds of social organization. There is frequent personal contact with the labour and union movement, enabling a direct exchange of ideas, objectives and practices prevailing in both movements. The new groupings therefore complement the classic organizational structures of political parties and unions. They also may be said to form an informal part of the labour movement as a whole, the problems and objectives of which may therefore be carried to sectors of the population not normally associated with it.

The paradox of simultaneous restoration in, and radicalization of, society is repeated in individual attitudes as the paradox between resignation and commitment. Since the Conservatives under Margaret Thatcher took office in May 1979, two important political shifts have taken place. Firstly, the Labour Party has gone to the left, and the traditional left wing of the Party has considerably changed its profile. The Tribune Group, the old focal point of the Party's Left, has undergone a *de facto* split. The new left wing of the Labour Party is now stronger and more radical than ever. Secondly, the Alliance of the Liberal and Social Democratic Parties has shaped a new bourgeois centre of British politics. Both of these developments are still incomplete. They have led to bitter internal arguments and struggles, and, despite its increased radicalization, rendered the labour movement somewhat incapable of acting. But this may only be temporary. There exists a perhaps contradictory situation in Britain today. The media-dominated public opinion seems more conservative and Atlanticist than during the 1970s, although both the Labour Party led by Neil Kinnock and the Liberal/SDP Alliance under David Steel and David Owen appear to have gained considerable ground as a result of the local elections and parliamentary by-elections held in 1985 and 1986. On the other hand, however, the potential for socialist changes in the population has grown. The 'ideological' shift to the right contrasts with a 'practical' shift to the left. Some of these contradictory tendencies overlap in the same personalities; a fact which makes the situation yet more paradoxical. During the Falklands War, for example, the then leader of the Labour Party, Michael Foot, and the then deputy leader (now Labour's Shadow Foreign Secretary), Denis Healey, both demanded negotiations to be mediated via the United Nations, but they never questioned the legitimacy and legality of British territorial claims over the Falkland

Islands. They thereby did not only express the opinion of a large majority of Labour voters, but also of many trade unionists. The present stagnation of the British labour movement has little to do with lack of ideas, plans or programmes. The 'Alternative Economic Strategy', for instance, clearly shows some liveliness of discussion. This stagnation has more to do with the incapacity of the labour movement so far to break with traditions which belong to the past Empire or the present class-ridden society, and to liberate itself from obsolete loyalties as well as outdated ways of thinking. Structures which have developed organically, like the British institutions, exercise great power and influence—in this Gordian knot lies both the strength, and the weakness, of the British labour movement.

APPENDIX

THE BIG HEWER

Voice (First Miner)   As my old mother used to say to me, what's bred in the bone, you cannot knock out of the flesh.

Unaccompanied guitar

Voice (Second Miner)   As my father told me, get all your tools and as the manager is approaching you now and he is asking your name, reply sharply with your name and stand on your toes—show that you are willing to work. And that's what my father advised me.

First Song (First Singer)
> Schoolday's over, come on then John
> Time to be gettin' your pit boots on
> On with your sark and moleskin trousers
> Time you was on your way
> Time you was learning the pitman's job
> And earning the pitman's pay.

(The melody is taken up by a guitar and forms the background to the voice.)

Voice (Third Miner)   I was fourteen when I first went down the mine. November 5th, Guy Fawkes Day, on a Monday.

(A guitar takes over and then continues smoothly into the song.)

Second Song (Second Singer)
> Come on then Jim, it's time to go
> Time you was working down below
> Time to be handling a pick and shovel
> You start at the pit today
> Time you was learning the collier's job
> And earning a collier's pay.

(The melody is taken up by a fiddle and forms the background to the voice.)

Voice (Fourth Miner)   I was twelve when I left school and soon as I reached the age of fourteen I went to the pit. The pit was the place.

Third Song (Third Singer)
> Come on then Dai
> It's almost light
> Time you was off to the anthracite
> The morning mist is in the valley
> It's time you was on your way
> Time you was learning the miner's job
> And earnin' the miner's pay.

(The melody is taken up by an accordion and forms the background to the voice.)

Voice (Fifth Miner)   When I was a boy we all thought of the mines. When I was in school I used to parade wearing my long trousers and parading with my naked lamp on the road in the night as colliers months before I had the job you see. Oh yes.

Unaccompanied accordion

Spoken song, interrupted by a banjo

First Singer: Come on then John

Second Singer: Way, Ay

Third Singer: Righto

First Singer: Off you go today
> Off you go to earn your pay
> In the mine lad.

(A bassoon plays.)

Voice (Sixth Miner)   You know, I'll never forget that day, never will, not as long as I live.

First Singer: Now don't be late
> You've got your bait
> You've got your cold tea
> In the bottle
> Now you're every inch a miner

(Instrumental)

Voice (Seventh Miner)   My mother didn't want me to go to the pit.

Second Singer: You're a miner
Chorus   You're a pitman, you're a collier
                You're a miner.

Voice (Eighth Miner)   I hated it, I hated it the first day I went
there.

(MacColl, 1962)

BIBLIOGRAPHY

Aaronovitch, Sam and Smith, Ron: *The Political Economy of British Capitalism. A Marxist Analysis*, Maidenhead 1981

Adlam, Diana et al.: *Politics and Power*, Vol. I: *New Perspectives on Socialist Politics*, Vol. II: *Problems in Labour Politics*, London 1980

Allen, V.L.: *The militancy of British Miners*, Baildon Green, Shipley 1981

Allison, Lincoln: *Condition of England: Essays and Impressions*, London 1981

Anning, N. and Wintour, P.: *The raids: was it revenge?*, New Statesman, 24 July 1981

Arnold, Guy: *The Unions*, London 1981

Aughey, Arthur and Norton, Phillip: *Conservatives and Conservatism*, London 1981

Bailey, Brian: *The Industrial Heritage of Britain*, London 1982

Baker, Chris and Caldwell, Peter: *Unions and change since 1945*, London 1982

Barnsby, George J.: *Social conditions in the Black Country 1800–1900*, Wolverhampton 1980

Beer, Samuel H.: *Britain Against Itself: The Political Contradictions of Collectivism*, London 1982

Behrens, Robert: *The Conservative Party from Heath to Thatcher. Policies and Politics 1974–1979*, Westmead, Farnborough 1980

Bell, Quentin: *A New Noble School: The Pre-Raphaelites*, London 1982

Black, John: *The Economics of Modern Britain*, Oxford 1980

Bohrer, Karl Heinz: *Ein bißchen Lust am Untergang. Englische Ansichten*, Munich 1979

Bourne, Richard: *Londoners*, London 1981

Bradby, Davis; James, Louis and Sharrat, Bernard: *Performance and Politics in Popular Drama: Aspects of Popular Entertainment in Theatre, Film and Television 1800–1976*, Cambridge, 1980

Bradley, Ian: *Breaking the Mould? The Birth and Prospect of the Social Democratic Party*, Oxford 1981

— *The Middle Classes are alive and kicking*, London 1982

Brent, Peter: *Charles Darwin. A Man of Enlarged Curiosity*, London

1981

Brewer, John and Styles, John (Ed.): *An ungovernable People: the English and their Law in the 17th and 18th century*, London 1979

British Corporate Leaders: a Profile. A Korn/Ferry International Study, London 1982

Brockway, Lucile H.: *Science and Colonial Expansion. The Role of the British Royal Botanic Gardens*, London 1979

Brown, William (Ed.): *The Changing Contours of British Industrial Relations*, Oxford 1980

Buck, Philip W. (Ed.): *How Conservatives Think*, Harmondsworth 1975

Burgess, Keith: *The Challenge of Labour. Shaping British Society 1850-1930*, London 1980

Burnet, Alastair and Landels, Willie: *The Time of Our Lives. A pictorial history of Britain since 1945*, London 1981

Burnett, T.A.J.: *The Rise and Fall of a Regency Dandy. The Life and Times of Scrope Berdmore Davies*, London 1981

Butler, David and Sloman, Anne: *British Political Facts 1900-79*, London 1980

Butlin, Martin: *The Paintings and Drawings of William Blake*, London and New Haven 1981

Cannadine, David: *Lords and Landlords. The Aristocracy and the Towns 1774-1967*, Leicester 1980

Caufield, Catherine: *The Emperor of the United States of America and other magnificent British Eccentrics*, London 1981

Césaire, Aimé: *Discours sur le Colonialisme*, Paris 1973 (1955)

Chancellor, E. Beresford: *Memorials of St. James's Street. Together with the Annals of Almack's*, London 1922

Charlesworth, Andrew: *An Atlas of Rural Protest in Britain*, London 1982

Clarke, Sebastian: *Jah Music. The Evolution of the Popular Jamaican Song*, London 1980

Clegg, H.A.: *The Changing System of Industrial Relations in Great Britain*, Oxford 1979

Coates, Ken (Ed.): *What went wrong. Exploring the Fall of the Labour Government*, Nottingham 1979

–/ Silburn, Richard: *Poverty: The Forgotten Englishmen*, Harmondsworth 1970

–/ Topham, Tony: *Trade Unions in Britain*, Nottingham 1980

Cole, David: *The Work of Sir Gilbert Scott*, London 1980

Colson, Percy: *White's 1693–1950 (White's Club)*, London 1951

Communist Party (Ed.): *Power & Prejudice = Racism*. Communist Party Discussion Pack, London 1980

— *Black & Blue. Racism and the Police*, Communist Party Pamphlet, London 1981

Conference of Socialist Economists, London Working Group: *The Alternative Economic Strategy. A Labour Movement Response to the Economic Crisis*, London 1980

Cook, Chris and Taylor, Ian: *The Labour Party. An introduction to its history, structure and politics*, London 1980

Cottle, Thomas: *Black Testimony. The Voices of Britain's West Indians*, London 1978

Cowling, Maurice: *Religion and Public Doctrine in Modern England*, Cambridge 1980

Cronin, James E. and Schneer, Jonathan: *Social Conflict and Political Order in Modern Britain*, London 1982

Crozier, Brian: *The Minimum State*, London 1980

Dahrendorf, Ralf: *On Britain*, London 1982

— *England ist keine Idylle. Eine Diskussion über Großbritannien und Deutschland*, Die Zeit, 3 August 1979, p. 4

Dallas, Karl: *One Hundred Songs of Toil. 450 years of workers' songs*, London 1974

Darwin, B.: *British Clubs*, London 1943

Dash, Jack: *Good Morning, Brothers! A militant trade unionist's frank autobiography*, London 1970

Davis, Stephen and Simon, Peter: *Reggae Blooklines. In Search of the Music and Culture of Jamaica*, London 1977

Debrett's Etiquette and Modern Manners, ed. by Elsie Burch Donald, London 1981

Debrett's Handbook, London 1981

Department of the Environment (Drake, M; O'Brien, M. and Biebuyck, T.): *Single and Homeless*, London 1981

Dhondy, Farrukh: *East End at Your Feet*, London 1976

— and Beese, Barbara and Hassan, Leila: *The Black Explosion in British Schools*, London 1982

Donnison, David: *The Politics of Poverty*, Oxford 1982

Dunleavy, Patrick: *The Politics of Mass Housing in Britain 1945–1975*, Oxford 1982

Eaton, Jack and Gill, Colin: *The Trade Union Directory*, London 1981

English Centre (Bennett, Sh.; Grant, P.; Griffin, G.; Scott, L.; Smith, C.E.; Yearwood, Ph.): *West Indian Poetry*, London n.d.

Ereira, Alan: *The People's England*, London 1980

Esher, Lionel: *A Broken Wave: The Rebuilding of England 1940–1980*, London 1981

Fagin, Leonard: *Unemployment and Health in Families. Case studies based on family interviews. A Pilot Study*, Department of Health and Social Security, London 1981

Falconer, Keith: *A guide to England's industrial heritage*, London 1980

Field, Frank: *Inequality in Britain. Freedom, Welfare and the State*, Glasgow 1981

– *Poverty 'has doubled under Thatcher'*, the *Guardian*, 12 May 1986, p. 3

File, Nigel and Power, Chris: *Black Settlers in Britain 1555–1958*, London 1981

Findlater, Richard (E.): *At the Royal Court. 25 years of the English Stage Company*, Ambergate 1981

Fine, Ben: *Economic Theory and Ideology*, London 1980

Finer, S.E.: *The Changing British Party System 1945–1979*, Washington D.C. 1980

Fisher, Nigel: *The Tory Leaders. Their struggle for power*, London 1977

Florey, R.A.: *The General Strike of 1926. The Economic, Political and Social Causes of that Class War*, London 1980

Foot, Michael: *Debts of Honour*, London 1980

– *Loyalists and Loners*, London 1986

Foot, Paul: *Immigration and Race in British Politics*, Harmondsworth 1965

Friend, Andrew and Metcalf, Andy: *Slump city: the politics of mass unemployment*, London 1981

Galsworthy, John: *A Modern Comedy*, London 1958 (1929)

Gamble, Andrew: *Britain in Decline. Economic Policy, Political Strategy and the British State*, London 1981

Garrison, Len: *Black Youth. Rastafarianism and the Identity Crisis in Britain*, London 1979

Gilmour, Robin: *The Idea of the Gentleman in the Victorian Novel*,

London 1981

Girouard, Mark: *The Return to Camelot, Chivalry and the English Gentleman*, New Haven and London 1981

Girtin, Tom: *The Abominable Clubman*, London 1964

Goldthorpe, John H.: *The affluent worker*, Cambridge 1968

– *Social mobility and class structure in modern Britain*, Oxford 1980

Goorney, Howard: *The Theatre Workshop Story*, London 1981

– and MacColl, Ewan (Eds.): *Agit-prop to Theatre Workshop: political playscripts, 1930–50*, Manchester 1986

Gorman, John: *To build Jerusalem. A photographic remembrance of British working class life*, London 1980

Graves, Charles: *Leather armchairs: the Chivas Regal book of London Clubs*, London 1963

Griffin, Brian and Smith, Richard: *Power: British Management in Focus*, London 1982

Grimble, Ian: *Regency People*, London 1972

Halsey, A.H.; Heath, A.F.; Ridge, J.M.: *Origins and Destinations: Family, Class and Education in Modern Britain*, Oxford 1980

Harsch, Ernest: *US Intervention in Jamaica. How Washington Toppled the Manley Government*, New York 1981

Haseler, Stephen: *The Tragedy of Labour*, Oxford 1982

Hayes, John and Nuhman, Peter: *Understanding the Unemployed: the psychological effects of unemployment*, London 1981

Heley, E.W.: *Philosophy: Beyond Expediency*; in: Tertiary (Cotterell, A.B. & Heley, E.W.), Cheltenham 1981

History Today, Vol. 31, Sept. 1981: *The History of Blacks in Britain*, London 1981

Hobsbawm, Eric et al.: *The Forward March of Labour Halted?* London 1981

Hodgson, Geoff: *Labour at the crossroads*, Oxford 1981

Hoggart, Simon and Leigh, D.: *Michael Foot. A Portrait*, London 1981

Holme, R.K.: *Inner City Regeneration*, London 1982

Hood, Christopher and Wright, Maurice: *Big Government in Hard Times*, Oxford 1981

Hughes, John: *Britain in crisis: De-Industrialisation and How to Fight it*, Nottingham 1982

Humphreys, A.L.: *Crockford's or the Goddess of Chance in St. James's Street 1828–1844*, London 1953

Husband, Charles (Ed.): *Race in Britain. Continuity and Change*, London 1982
Hutchinson, T.W.: *The Philosophy and Politics of Economics*, Oxford 1981

Institute of Race Relations (ed): *Police against Black people*, Race & Class No. 6, London 1979
− *Britain 81, Rebellion and Repression*, Race & Class Vol. XXIII No. 2/3, London 1981
Itzin, Catherine: *Stages in the Revolution. Political Theatre in Britain since 1968*, London 1981

James, C.L.R.: *An accumulation of blunders, New Society*, 3 Dec. 1981
Jenkins, Hugh: *Rank and File*, London 1980
Johnson, Linton Kwesi: *Dread, Beat and Blood*, London 1975
− *Inglan is a bitch*, London 1980
Johnson, Paul: *The imbalance of power, Times Literary Supplement*, 8 Oct. 1982
Jones, Greta: *Social Darwinism and English Thought*, Brighton 1980
Jones, Lewis: *Cwmardy*, London 1980
Joseph, Keith and Sumption, Jonathan: *Equality*, London 1979
Jost, Stephan: *Person und Politik von Shirley Williams M.P., Frankfurter Hefte*, Frankfurt, November 1982

Kasterine, Dimitri: *England and the English*, Kingswood, Tadworth 1981
Keay, John: *Eccentric Travellers*, London 1982
Kennedy, Paul: *The realities behind diplomacy: Background influence on British External Policy 1965–1980*, London 1980
King, Martin Luther: *Where Do We Go From Here: Chaos or Community?*, New York, 1967
− *The Words of Martin Luther King, Jr. (Selected and Introduced by Coretta Scott King)*, London 1984 (New York 1983)
Kramnick, Isaac (Ed.): *Is Britain Dying? Perspectives on the Current Crisis*, London 1979

Labour Research Department, *Unfair Shares. Rich and Poor in Britain Today*, London 1981
Lamming, George: *The Emigrants*, London 1980 (1954)
Layton-Henry, Zig (Ed.): *Conservative Party Politics*, London 1980

Leighton, Martin: *Men at Work*, London 1981

Lejeune, Anthony: *The Gentlemen's Clubs of London*, London 1979

Lessing, Doris: *Canopus in Argos: Archives* Vol. One: *Re-Colonised Planet 5 Shikasta*, London 1979; Vol. Two: *The Marriages between Zones Three, Four and Five*, London 1980; Vol. Three: *The Sirian Experiments*, London 1981; Vol. Four: *The Making of the Representative for Planet 8*, London 1982

Lichtenberg, Georg Christoph: *Schriften und Briefe*, Band 3, Munich 1972

Lloyd, A.L.: *Come all ye bold miners. Ballads & Songs of the Coalfields*, London 1978

– *Folksong in England*, London 1967

MacColl, Ewan and Parker, Charles: *The Ballad of John Axon*, Argo-Record RG 474, 1958

– *The Big Hewer*, Argo-Record DA 140, 1962

MacGregor, Susan: *The Politics of Poverty*, London 1982

Mack, Joanna: *Schools for privilege*, New Society, 7 July 1977

Manifesto: *A radical strategy for Britain's future*, London 1981

Mangan, J.A.: *Athleticism in the Victorian and Edwardian Public School*, Cambridge 1981

Manley, Michael: *A paradox for the creatures of Empire, The Guardian*, 21 July 1981, p. 9

Martin, Ross M.: *TUC: The Growth of a Pressure Group 1868–1976*, Oxford 1980

Marwick, Arthur: *Class: Image and Reality in Britain, France and the USA since 1930*, London 1980

Mayhew, Henry: *London Labour and the London Poor*, London 1851

Mason, Philip: *The English Gentleman. The rise and fall of an ideal*, London 1982

McCord, Norman: *Strikes*, Oxford 1980

McGrath, John: *A Good Night Out. Popular Theatre: Audience, Class and Form*, London 1981

Middlemas, Keith: *Politics in Industrial Society. The Experience of the British System since 1911*, London 1979

Miles, R. and Phizacklea, A.: *Racism and political action in Britain*, London 1979

Moore, Sheila: *The Conservative Party*, Feltham 1980

National Union of Mineworkers: *Rules, Model Rules, Standing Orders*, London 1978

Nevill, Ralph: *London Clubs. Their history and treasures*, London 1911

Newby, Howard: *Green and Pleasant Land? Social Change in Rural England*, London 1979

Norgate, Mathew and Wykes, Alan: *Not so savage (Savage Club)*, London 1976

Orwell, George: *Down and Out in Paris and London*, London 1933

Owens, Joseph: *Dread. The Rastafarians of Jamaica*, London 1979 (1976)

Paley, Morton D.: *William Blake*, Oxford 1978

Palmer, Roy: *A ballad history of England from 1588 to the present day*, London 1979

— *Poverty Knock: A picture of industrial life in the 19th century through songs, ballads and contemporary accounts*, Cambridge 1974

Pollard, Sidney: *The Wasting of the British Economy*, London 1982

Powell, Anthony: *A Dance to the Music of Time*, London 1951–75.

Powell, Enoch: *Mr. Powell urges a policy of repatriation*, The Times, 5 Oct. 1976

— *Powell speech 'raises risk of race war'*, Daily Telegraph, 30 March 1981

Prescod-Roberts, Margaret and Steele, Norma: *Black Women: Bringing it All Back Home*, Bristol 1980

Rae, John: *The Public School Revolution. Britain's Independent Schools 1964–79*, London 1981

Raven, Jon: *Songs of a Changing World*, London 1972

— *Victoria's Inferno, songs of the old mills, mines, manufactories, canals and railways*, Tettenhall, Wolverhampton 1978

Raven, Simon: *The English Gentleman. An essay in attitudes*, London 1961

Röder, Karl-Heinz: *Das politische System Großbritanniens. Geschichte und Gegenwart*, Cologne 1982

Rogers, Colin: *The Battle of Stepney. The Sidney Street Siege: Its Causes and Consequences*, London 1981

Rose, Dennis: *Life, Times and recorded Works of Robert Dighton (1752-1814). Actor, Artist and Printseller and Three of his Artist*

Sons, Tisbury, Salisbury 1981

Royle, Edward: *Radicals, Secularists and Republicans: Popular free-thought in Britain 1866–1915*, Manchester 1980

Rubinstein, W.D.: *Men of Property. The very wealthy in Britain since the Industrial Revolution*, London 1981

Runnymede Trust and the Radical Statistics Race Group: *Britain's Black Population*, London 1980

Russel, T.: *The Tory Party. Its Politics, Divisions and Future*, Harmondsworth 1978

Salkey, Andrew: *Danny Jones*, London 1980

Samuel, Raphael (Ed.): *People's History and Socialist Theory*, London 1981

Sampson, Anthony: *The Changing Anatomy of Britain*, London 1982

Scarman, Lord: *The Brixton Disorders 10–12 April 1981*, Report of an Inquiry by the Rt Hon The Lord Scarman, HMSO, London 1981

Scruton, Roger: *The Meaning of Conservatism*, London 1980

Seabrook Jeremy: *Unemployment*, London 1982

– *What went wrong? Working People and the Ideals of the Labour Movement*, London 1978

Selvon, Samuel: *The Lonely Londoners*, London 1979 (1956)

Shaw, George Bernhard: *Maxims for Revolutionists*, in: Collected Plays with their prefaces, Vol. II, Man and Superman, London 1971

Sivanandan, A.: *A Different Hunger. Writings on Black Resistance*, London 1982

Smith, Leo and Jones, David (Ed.): *Deprivation, Participation, and Community Action*, London 1981

Smythe-Palmer, A.: *The Ideal of a Gentleman or a mirror for Gentlefolks. A Portrayal in Literature from the Earliest Times*, London 1908

Spender, Humphrey: *Worktown People: Photographs from Northern England 1937–38*, Bristol 1982

Stafford, G.B.: *The End of Economic Growth?* Oxford 1981

State Research: *Review of Security and the State 1980*, London 1980

Stephenson, Hugh: *Mrs. Thatcher's First Year*, London 1980

Sutcliffe, David: *British Black English*, Oxford 1982

Sutherland, Douglas: *The English Gentleman*, London 1978

Tawney, R. H.: *Equality*, London 1931

Taylor, John: *Working Men's Clubs. History Workshop*, London 1972

Taylor, Robert: *The Fifth Estate. Britain's Unions in the Seventies*, London 1978

Thackeray, W.M.: *The Book of Snobs*, London 1848

Thelwell, Michael: *The Harder They Come*, London 1980

Thompson, E.P.: *Out of Apathy*, London 1960

– *The Making of the English Working Class*, Harmondsworth 1979 (1963)

– *An open letter to Leszek Kolakowski*, in: The Socialist Register 1973, London 1974

– *William Morris. Romantic to Revolutionary*, New York 1977 (1955)

– *Das Elend der Theorie. Zur Produktion geschichtlicher Erfahrung*, Frankfurt/New York 1980 (original British edition 1978)

– *Protest and Survive*, Harmondsworth 1980

– *E.P. Thompson, The Times*, 3 Aug. 1981

Tilly, Louise A. and Charles: *Class Conflict and Collective Action*, London 1981

Timbs, John: *Clubs and Club Life in London. With anecdotes of its famous coffee-houses, hostelries and taverns, from the seventeenth century to the present time*, London 1872

Townsend, Peter: *Poverty in the United Kingdom: A survey of household resources and standards of living*, Harmondsworth 1979

– *Poverty in the 80s, New Socialist* Sept./Oct. 1981, pp. 25–31

– /Abel-Smith, Brian: *The Poor and the Poorest*, London 1965

Tremlett, George: *The First Century. The exciting saga of the Working Men's Club & Institute Union*, London 1962

Undy, R.; Ellis, V.; McCarthy, W.F.J.; Halmos, A.M.: *Change in Trade Unions*, London 1981

Verne, Jules: *Around the World in Eighty Days*, translated from the French by I.O. Evans, London 1967

Vogeler, A.: *The Graphic Works by George Cruikshank*, London 1979

Voices 23, Winter 1981. Federation of Worker Writers and Community Publishers, Manchester 1981

Voltaire: *Letters on England*, translated with an introduction by

L. Tancock, Harmondsworth 1980

Warde, Alan: *Consensus and Beyond. The development of Labour Party Strategy*, Manchester 1982

Watkins, Michael: *The English. The Countryside and its People*, London 1981

Waugh, Evelyn: *Brideshead Revisited*, London 1960 (1945)

Waugh, Francis, Gledstanes: *The Athenaeum Club and its associations*, Reprint The Athenaeum 1968

Weerth, Georg: *Weerths Werke in zwei Bänden*, Berlin and Weimar 1974

West, Richard: *An English Journey*, London 1981

Wiener, Martin J.: *English Culture and the Decline of the Industrial Spirit 1850–1980*, Cambridge 1981

Wilkinson, Tony: *Down and Out*, London 1981

Williams, Raymond: *Culture and Society 1780–1950*, London 1958
– *Essays in Cultural Materialism*, London 1980

Williams, Shirley: *Politics is for People*, Penguin Books, Harmondsworth 1981
– *A Job to Live. The Impact of Tomorrow's Technology on Work and Society*, Penguin Books, Harmondsworth 1985
– *Searching Answer to the Employment Crisis*, the *Guardian*, 28 February 1986, p. 9

Winchester, Simon: *Their Noble Lordships. The hereditary peerage today*, London 1981

Wood, Christopher: *The Pre-Raphaelites*, London 1981

Working Lives, Centerprise Trust, London 1977

INDEX